MCSE Test Success:
Windows 95

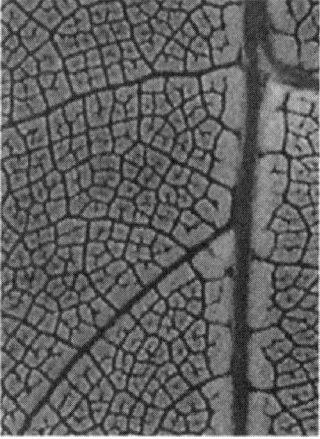

MCSE Test Success™:
Windows® 95

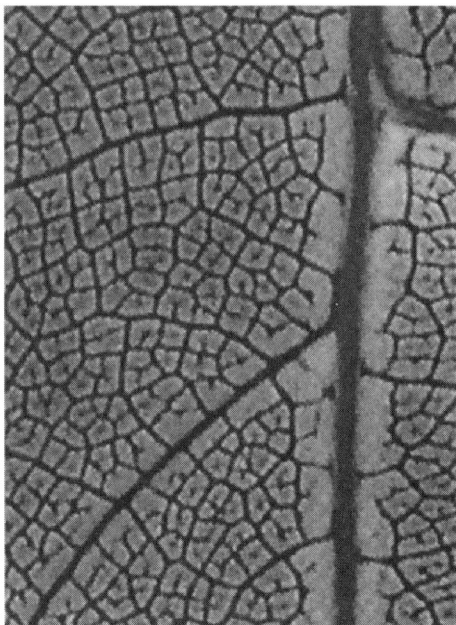

VFX Technologies, Inc.

NETWORK PRESS ® SYBEX

San Francisco • Paris • Düsseldorf • Soest

Associate Publisher: Guy Hart-Davis
Contracts and Licensing Manager: Kristine Plachy
Acquisitions & Developmental Editor: Bonnie Bills
Editor: Kim Wimpsett
Technical Editor: Jim Cooper
Book Designers: Patrick Dintino, Bill Gibson
Graphic Illustrator: Michael Gushard
Electronic Publishing Specialist: Bill Gibson
Production Coordinator: Amy Eoff
Indexer: Rebecca Plunkett
Cover Designer: Archer Design
Cover Illustrator/Photographer: FPG International

Screen reproductions produced with Collage Complete.

Collage Complete is a trademark of Inner Media Inc.

SYBEX, Network Press, and the Network Press logo are registered trademarks of SYBEX Inc.

Test Success is a trademark of SYBEX Inc.

TRADEMARKS: SYBEX has attempted throughout this book to distinguish proprietary trademarks from descriptive terms by following the capitalization style used by the manufacturer.

Library of Congress Card Number: 98-84539
ISBN: 0-7821-2252-3

Manufactured in the United States of America

10 9 8 7 6 5 4 3 2 1

November 1, 1997

Dear SYBEX Customer:

Microsoft is pleased to inform you that SYBEX is a participant in the Microsoft® Independent Courseware Vendor (ICV) program. Microsoft ICVs design, develop, and market self-paced courseware, books, and other products that support Microsoft software and the Microsoft Certified Professional (MCP) program.

To be accepted into the Microsoft ICV program, an ICV must meet set criteria. In addition, Microsoft reviews and approves each ICV training product before permission is granted to use the Microsoft Certified Professional Approved Study Guide logo on that product. This logo assures the consumer that the product has passed the following Microsoft standards:

- The course contains accurate product information.
- The course includes labs and activities during which the student can apply knowledge and skills learned from the course.
- The course teaches skills that help prepare the student to take corresponding MCP exams.

Microsoft ICVs continually develop and release new MCP Approved Study Guides. To prepare for a particular Microsoft certification exam, a student may choose one or more single, self-paced training courses or a series of training courses.

You will be pleased with the quality and effectiveness of the MCP Approved Study Guides available from SYBEX.

Sincerely,

Holly Heath
ICV Account Manager
Microsoft Training & Certification

MICROSOFT INDEPENDENT COURSEWARE VENDOR PROGRAM

Acknowledgments

The name on the cover is only one part of the group involved in creating this book. I'd like to thank my family (both human and feline) for their support while I was working on this project. (Well, Scott, the human part of the family, was supportive. The three feline members tried to sleep on the keyboard while I was working and had to be restrained.)

I'd also like to thank the crew at Sybex for their suggestions on how to make this book even better, particularly Bonnie Bills, Kim Wimpsett, and Jim Cooper. And finally, thanks to Doug Archell for putting me in touch with Sybex for this project in the first place.

Contents at a Glance

Table of Contents

Introduction

Onee of the greatest challenges facing corporate America today is finding people who are qualified to manage corporate computer networks. Many companies have Microsoft networks, which run Windows 95, Windows NT, and other Microsoft BackOffice products (such as Microsoft SQL Server and Systems Management Server).

Microsoft developed its Microsoft certification program to certify those people who have the skills to work with Microsoft products and networks. The most highly coveted certification is MCSE, or Microsoft Certified Systems Engineer.

Why become an MCSE? You will have much greater earning potential with this certification, as an MCSE carries high industry recognition. Certification can be your key to a new job or a higher salary—or both.

So what's stopping you? If it's because you don't know what to expect from the tests or are worried you might not pass, then this book is for you.

Your Key to Passing Exam 70-064

This book provides you with the key to passing Exam 70-064, Implementing and Supporting Windows 95. Inside, you'll find *all* the information relevant to this exam, including hundreds of practice questions, designed to make sure you are ready for even the picky questions about less frequently used options.

Understand the Exam Objectives

To help you prepare for certification exams, Microsoft provides a list of objectives for each test. This book is structured according to the Exam 70-064 objectives, which measure your ability to design, administer, and troubleshoot Windows 95.

At-a-glance review sections and hundreds of study questions bolster your knowledge of the information relevant to each objective and the exam itself. You learn exactly what you need to know without wasting time on background material or detailed explanations.

This book prepares you for the exam in the shortest amount of time possible—although to be ready for the real world, you need to study the subject in greater depth and get a good deal of hands-on practice.

Get Ready for the Real Thing

More than 150 sample test questions prepare you for the test-taking experience. These are multiple-choice questions that resemble actual exam questions—some are even more difficult than what you'll find on the exam. If you can pass the Sample Tests at the end of each unit and the Final Review in Unit 7, you'll know you're ready.

Is This Book for You?

This book is intended for those who already have some experience with Windows 95. It is especially well suited for:

- Students using courseware or taking a class to prepare for the exam, and who need to supplement their study material with test-based practice questions.

- Network engineers who have worked with the product but want to make sure there are no gaps in their knowledge.

- Anyone who has studied for the exams—by using self-study guides, by participating in computer-based training or classes, or by getting on-the-job experience—and wants to make sure that they're adequately prepared.

Understanding Microsoft Certification

Microsoft offers several levels of certification for anyone who has or is pursuing a career as a network professional working with Microsoft products:

- Microsoft Certified Professional (MCP)

- Microsoft Certified Systems Engineer (MCSE)

- Microsoft Certified Professional + Internet (MCP+I)

- Microsoft Certified Systems Engineer + Internet (MCSE+I)

- Microsoft Certified Trainer (MCT)

The level you choose depends on your area of expertise and your career goals.

Microsoft Certified Professional (MCP)

This certification is for individuals with expertise in one specific area. MCP certification is often a stepping stone to MCSE certification and allows you some benefits of Microsoft certification after just one exam.

By passing one core exam (meaning an operating system exam), you become an MCP.

Microsoft Certified Systems Engineer (MCSE)

For network professionals, the MCSE certification requires commitment. You need to complete all of the steps required for certification. Passing the exams shows you meet the high standards that Microsoft has set for MCSEs. To become an MCSE, you must pass a series of six exams:

1. Networking Essentials (waived for Novell CNEs) (70-058)

2. Implementing and Supporting Microsoft Windows 95 (70-064) *or* Implementing and Supporting Windows NT Workstation 4.0 (70-073)

3. Implementing and Supporting Microsoft Windows NT Server 4.0 (70-067)

4. Implementing and Supporting Microsoft Windows NT Server 4.0 in the Enterprise (70-068)

5. Elective

6. Elective

Some of the electives include:

- Internetworking with Microsoft TCP/IP on Microsoft Windows NT 4.0 (70-059)

- Implementing and Supporting Microsoft Internet Information Server 4.0 (70-087)

- Implementing and Supporting Microsoft Proxy Server 2.0 (70-088)

- Implementing and Supporting Microsoft Exchange Server 5.5 (70-081)

- Implementing and Supporting Microsoft SNA Server 4.0 (70-085)

- Implementing and Supporting Microsoft Systems Management Server 1.2 (70-018)

- Implementing a Database Design on Microsoft SQL Server 6.5 (70-027)

- System Administration for Microsoft SQL Server 6.5 (70-026)

> For fast access to a complete list of all Microsoft certification exams and links to their exam-specific pages, go to http://www.microsoft.com/train_cert/html/exam.htm.

Microsoft Certified Trainer (MCT)

As an MCT, you can deliver Microsoft-certified courseware through official Microsoft channels.

The MCT certification is more costly than the other options, because in addition to passing the exams, it requires that you sit through the official Microsoft courses. You also need to submit an application to be approved by Microsoft. The number of exams you are required to pass depends on the number of courses you want to teach.

> For the most up-to-date certification information, visit Microsoft's Web site at http://www.microsoft.com/train_cert.

Preparing for the MCSE Exams

To prepare for the MCSE certification exams, you should try to work with the product as much as possible. In addition, you can learn about the products and exams from a variety of resources:

- You can take instructor-led courses.

- Online training is an alternative to instructor-led courses. This is a useful option for people who cannot find any courses in their area or who do not have the time to attend classes.

- If you prefer to use a book to help you prepare for the MCSE tests, you can choose from a wide variety of publications. These range from complete study guides (such as the Network Press *MCSE Study Guide* series, which covers the core MCSE exams and key electives) through test-preparedness books similar to this one.

After you have completed your courses, training, or study guides, you'll find the *MCSE Test Success* books an excellent resource for preparing you for the test. You will discover if you've got it covered or if you still need to fill some holes.

NOTE For more MCSE information, point your browser to the Sybex Web site, where you'll find information about the MCP program, job links, and descriptions of other quality titles in the Network Press line of MCSE-related books. Go to http://www.sybex.com/ and click on the MCSE logo.

Scheduling and Taking an Exam

Once you think you are ready to take an exam, call Sylvan Prometric Testing Centers at (800) 755-EXAM (755-3926). They'll tell you where to find the closest testing center. Before you call, get out your credit card; each exam costs $100.

You can schedule the exam for a time convenient for you. The exams are downloaded from Sylvan Prometric to the testing center, and you show up at your scheduled time and take the exam on a computer.

Once you complete the exam, you will know right away whether you have passed. At the end of the exam, you will receive a score report. It will list the six areas you were tested on and how you performed. If you pass the exam, you don't need to do anything else—Sylvan Prometric uploads the test results to Microsoft. If you don't pass, it's another $100 to schedule the exam again. But at least you will know from the score report where you did poorly, so you can study the areas in which you need work.

TIP You can also register online. To do so, go to http://www.prometric.com/ testingcandidates/register/reg.asp.

Test-Taking Hints

If you know what to expect, your chances of passing the exam will be much greater. The following are some tips that can help you achieve success.

Get there early and be prepared   This is your last chance to review. Bring your *MCSE Test Success* book and review any areas with which you are not comfortable.

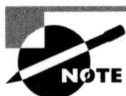

> If you need a quick drink of water or a visit to the restroom, take the time before the exam. Once your exam starts, it will not be paused for these needs.

When you arrive for your exam, you will be asked to present two forms of identification, one with a signature. You will also be asked to sign a piece of paper verifying that you understand the testing rules (for example, the rule that says you will not cheat on the exam).

Before you start the exam, you will have an opportunity to take a practice exam. It is not related to Windows 95 and is simply offered so you will have a feel for the exam process.

What you can and can't take in with you   These are closed-book exams. Many testing centers are very strict about what you can take into the testing room. Some centers even forbid you to bring in items like a zipped-up purse.

You will be able to take in scratch paper provided by the testing center. Use this paper as much as possible to diagram the questions. Many times diagramming questions will help make the answer clear. You will have to give this paper back to the test administrator at the end of the exam.

If you feel tempted to take in any outside material, beware that many testing centers use monitoring devices such as video and audio equipment. Prometric Testing Centers take the test-taking process and the test validation very seriously.

Test approach   As you take the test, if you know the answer to a question, fill it in and move on. If you're not sure of the answer, mark your best guess, then "mark" the question so that at the end of the exam you can review the questions you marked and check your answers.

At the end of the exam, you can review the questions. Depending on the amount of time remaining, you can then view all of the questions again, or you can view only the questions that you "marked." I always like to double-check all of my answers, just in case I misread any of the questions on the first pass. (Sometimes half of the battle is in trying to figure out exactly what the question is asking you.) Also, sometimes I find that a related question later in the exam provides a clue for a question about which I was uncertain.

> **TIP** Read carefully, as the questions seem to be phrased to be intentionally confusing. This is not the time to skim!

Remember: Answer all the questions. Unanswered questions are scored as incorrect and will count against you. Also, make sure you keep an eye on the remaining time so you can pace yourself accordingly.

> **TIP** Don't worry if you don't own a watch. A display in the upper-right corner of your testing monitor will display both the current time and the number of minutes you have left.

If you do not pass the exam, note everything you can remember while the exam is still fresh in your mind. This will help you prepare for your next try. Although the next exam will not be exactly the same, the questions will be similar, and you don't want to make the same mistakes.

After You Become Certified

Once you become an MCSE, Microsoft kicks in some goodies, including:

- A one-year subscription to Microsoft TechNet, a monthly subscription to CDs that contain Microsoft support information (including online versions of all product Resource Kits), service packs, utilities, and driver updates.

- A one-year subscription to the Microsoft Beta Evaluation program, which is a great way to get your hands on new software. Be the first kid on the block to play with new and upcoming operating systems and evaluations.

- Access to a secured area of the Microsoft Web site that provides technical support and product information. This certification benefit is also available for MCP certification.

- Permission to use the Microsoft Certified Professional logos (each certification has its own logo), which look great on letterhead and business cards.

- A certificate (you will get a certificate for each level of certification you reach).

- A one-year subscription to *Microsoft Certified Professional Magazine*, which provides information on professional and career development.

How to Use This Book

This book is designed to help you prepare for the MCSE exam. It reviews each objective and relevant test-taking information and offers you a chance to test your knowledge through study questions and sample tests.

The first six units in this book correspond to the Microsoft objectives groupings:

- Planning

- Installation and Configuration

- Configuring and Managing Resource Access

- Integration and Interoperability

- Monitoring and Optimization

- Troubleshooting

The seventh unit is the Final Review, which contains test questions pertaining to all the previous units.

For each unit:

1. Review the exam objectives at the beginning of the unit. (You may want to check the Microsoft Training Certification Web site at http://www.microsoft.com/Train_Cert/ to make sure the objectives haven't changed, as they're updated fairly often.)

TIP Check out Sybex's Web site at http://www.sybex.com for any updates to the book.

2. Read through or scan the reference material that follows the objectives list. Broken down according to the objectives, this section helps you brush up on the information you need to know for the exam.

3. Review your knowledge in the Study Questions section. These are straightforward questions designed to test your knowledge of the specific topic. Answers to Study Questions are listed in the Appendix at the back of the book.

4. Once you feel sure of your knowledge of the area, take the Sample Test at the end of the unit. The Sample Test's content and style matches the real exam. Set yourself a time limit based on the number of questions.

A general rule of thumb is that you should be able to answer 20 questions in 30 minutes.

5. When you've finished, check your answers with the Appendix in the back of the book. If you answer at least 85 percent of the questions correctly within the time limit (the first time you take the Sample Test), you're in good shape. To really prepare, you should note the questions you miss and be able to score 95 to 100 percent correctly on subsequent tries.

After you successfully complete Units 1–6:

1. You're ready for the Final Review in Unit 7. Allow yourself 90 minutes to complete the test. If you answer 85 percent of the questions correctly on the first try, you're well prepared. If not, go back and review your knowledge of the areas you struggled with, and take the test again.

2. Right before you take the test, scan the reference material at the beginning of each unit to refresh your memory.

At this point, you are well on your way to becoming certified!
Good Luck!

UNIT

1

Planning

Test Objectives: Planning

- Develop an appropriate implementation model for specific requirements in a Microsoft environment and a mixed Microsoft and NetWare environment. Considerations include:

  - Choosing a workgroup configuration or logging on to an existing domain

- Develop a security strategy in a Microsoft environment and a mixed Microsoft and NetWare environment. Strategies include:

  - System policies
  - User profiles
  - File and printer sharing

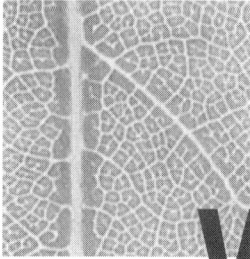

Windows 95 machines may be part of either a workgroup or a domain. Which option you choose will influence the types of security open to you and how that security may be implemented.

Choosing a Workgroup or Domain

From a Windows 95 network, you have the option of joining a domain (if in a client-server network with an Windows NT Primary Domain Controller) or joining a workgroup (if in a peer-to-peer network or one with NetWare servers). The differences between workgroups and domains are illustrated in Figure 1.1 and compared in Table 1.1.

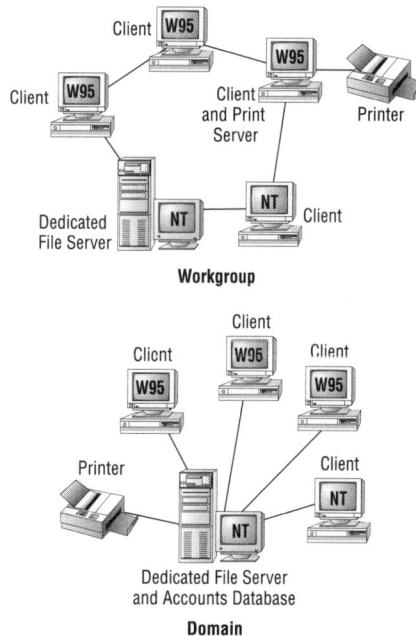

TABLE 1.1	Workgroup	Domain
Workgroups vs. Domains	A collection of computers logically grouped for the purpose of sharing resources	A collection of computers logically grouped around a common accounts database and security policy
	May assign share-level or user-level permissions	Only uses user-level permissions
	May incorporate Windows NT, Net-Ware, or Windows 95 computers	Must have a Windows NT Server to manage the accounts database
	Manages resources on a computer-level basis	Manages resources on a domain-level basis

Whether you join a workgroup or a domain depends on the way your network is set up. In either case, you'll need to provide the domain's or workgroup's unique name when requested. If you supply a domain name that does not already exist on your network, you'll get an error, but if you supply a workgroup name that does not already exist on the network, you'll create a new workgroup.

NOTE Domains cannot be created from a Windows 95 computer, as they are Windows NT constructs.

Developing a Security Strategy

Windows 95 is capable of supporting a three-part security system. This security can include any of the following:

- System policies
- User profiles
- File and printer sharing

System policies and profiles are two different ways of accomplishing the same task: defining how much control users have over the settings of their computers. Some differences between policies and profiles are outlined in Table 1.2.

	System Policies	User Profiles
TABLE 1.2 System Policies vs. User Profiles	Stored on the server	Stored locally or on the server
	Affect only a subset of user-based Registry information	Replace the entire contents of USER.DAT
	Implemented if user profiles are enabled	Implemented with a checkbox in the Passwords applet of the Control Panel
	Downloaded to user computer when user logs in	Loaded into Registry when user logs in

Figure 1.2 illustrates the differences in how system policies and user profiles may be implemented.

FIGURE 1.2

System policies vs. user profiles

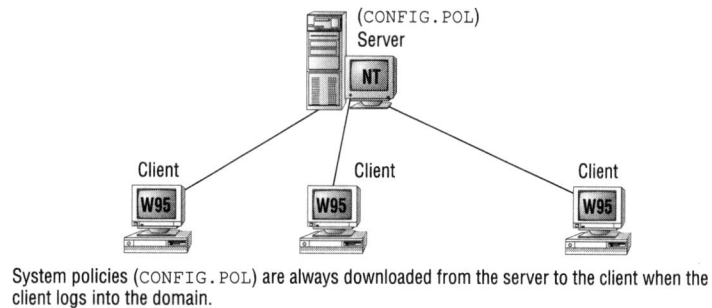

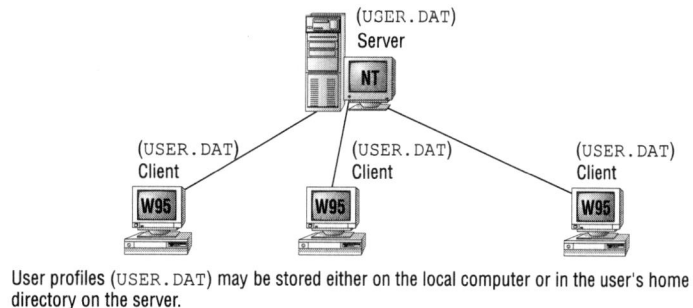

System policies (CONFIG.POL) are always downloaded from the server to the client when the client logs into the domain.

User profiles (USER.DAT) may be stored either on the local computer or in the user's home directory on the server.

File and printer sharing is a method of making files and printers accessible to other members of the workgroup.

System Policies

If you install the System Policy Editor found on the Windows 95 CD-ROM, you can set up policies governing the way users work with their computers.

> To install the System Policy Editor, insert the Windows 95 CD-ROM in the drive, activate the Add/Remove Programs applet in the Control Panel, move to the Windows Setup tab, and click the Have Disk button. The Policy Editor (POLEDIT) is located in ADMIN\APPTOOLS\ on the CD-ROM. You probably won't want to install this tool on most client computers.

System policies are stored in a CONFIG.POL file located on the server, rather than being stored locally as user profiles are. When users log into the server, the appropriate policies based on their User IDs will be downloaded to their computers, overwriting the contents of the Registry as needed.

You can create policies for both users and computers. Some user-specific policies include:

- Restricting access to the Control Panel
- Restricting access to printer settings
- Predefining Desktop settings
- Restricting access to network settings
- Restricting access to shell settings
- Restricting access to system tools such as the Registry Editor

System policies focus on how the computer functions on the network and how it presents itself to the user. System profiles could include one or more of the following:

- Enabling user-level security with pass-through validation to a server
- Creating a new logon banner
- Enabling participation in a workgroup or a domain

- Adjusting password caching and password requirements
- Settings for dial-up networking
- Disabling file and printer sharing

Whereas policies may be assigned to either a user or a machine, profiles are assigned to a user and activated when that user logs on.

NOTE   To assign policies to groups (as defined on the Primary Domain Controller) instead of just individual users, you must enable group policies on each computer you want to use them. Group policies are enabled from the Add/Remove Programs applet in the Control Panel.

To create a new policy, open the System Policy Editor (located in the System Tools subsection of the Accessories folder). You'll see a dialog box like the one shown in Figure 1.3.

FIGURE 1.3

Starting the System Policy Editor

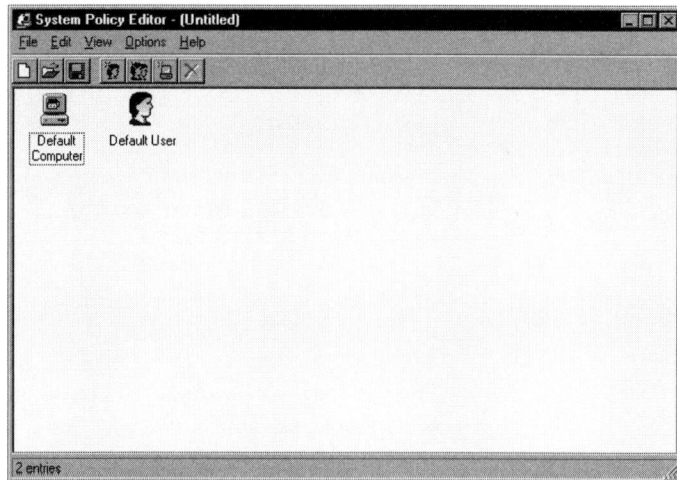

Security settings may be found in both the User and Computer settings, as described in Table 1.3.

T A B L E 1.3:   Security Settings Found in System Profiles

Setting	Description (When Set)	Location
Disable automatic NetWare login	Forces users to explicitly log onto NetWare servers	Computer/Microsoft Client for NetWare Networks
Disable file sharing	Prevents files from being shared from the local computer	Computer/File and Printer Sharing for Microsoft Networks
Disable file sharing controls	Negates any sharing controls in place	User/Sharing
Disable password caching	Forces users to log on each time	Computer/Password
Disable print sharing controls	Negates any sharing controls in place	User/Sharing
Disable printer sharing	Prevents printers from being shared from the local computer	Computer/File and Printer Sharing for Microsoft Networks
Disable Registry Editing tools	Prevents users from running `REGEDIT.EXE`	User/Restrictions
Disable SAP advertising	Prevents the computer from advertising its resources on a NetWare network	Computer/File and Printer Sharing for NetWare Networks
Don't show last user at logon	Shows a blank logon screen. Keeps people from guessing a previous user's password	Computer/Logon
Enable User Profiles	Enables user profiles (required to use system policies)	Computer/User Profiles
Hide share passwords with asterisks	Prevents share passwords from being displayed onscreen	Computer/Password
Log onto Windows NT	Allows you to specify a domain to log onto and permits you to disable network password caching	Computer/Microsoft Client for Windows Networks

T A B L E 1.3: Security Settings Found in System Profiles *(continued)*

Setting	Description (When Set)	Location
Minimum Windows password length	Sets a minimum length for Windows logon (does not affect network logon length) to make it more difficult to guess passwords	Computer/Password
Require alphanumeric password	Requires users to use passwords with letters and numbers	Computer/Password
Require validation for Windows access	Does not permit users to use Windows unless they log onto the network. Essentially, restricts machine access to those with user accounts	Computer/Logon
Restrict Network Control Panel	Prevents users from accessing specified parts of the Network applet	User/Control Panel
Restrict Passwords Control Panel	Prevents users from accessing specified parts of the Passwords applet	User/Control Panel

To edit system policies or create a new set, open the System Policy Editor (Select Start ➢ Run and type **POLEDIT.EXE**). You have the choice of running the System Policy Editor in Registry Mode or in Policy File Mode. Registry Mode directly edits the settings in the HKEY_LOCAL_MACHINE or HKEY_LOCAL_USER branches of Registry on the local or remote computer, making those changes take place immediately. Changes made in Policy File Mode affect only the policy file and do not take effect until the user next logs on.

To edit policy files, choose File ➢ New (or File ➢ Open) to open a policy file. When you open the file (which will appear in a Properties dialog box), you'll notice that the checkboxes next to the options may be in one of three states:

- Checked
- Unchecked
- Gray

The checked and unchecked boxes enable and disable options, respectively. Grayed-out boxes indicate that the setting is unchanged from the last time the user logged on, and no setting exists to force a change. Thus, CONFIG.POL only updates those settings that are explicitly configured, rather than all settings.

If a setting requires further information, then an edit control will appear at the bottom of the Properties dialog box when it's checked. For example, if you choose a minimum password length, then you'll need to supply that length.

User Profiles

Windows 95 user profiles define options and settings on a per-user basis, allowing users to maintain the same settings wherever they log in. User profiles cover everything in the HKEY_CURRENT_USER branch of the Registry and include the following:

- Control Panel settings for the Windows 95 user interface, including the font and colors used in the display, Desktop shortcuts, contents of folders, and the like

- Settings for persistent network connections and a record of recently used resources

- Application settings for applications that can write directly to the Registry (32-bit applications)

The user profile consists of the following:

- A USER.DAT file and its backup (USER.DA0)

- A Desktop folder

- A Recent folder

- A Start menu folder

- A Program folder

These folders are stored in the Profiles folder of the Windows 95 installation. Each time the user logs onto the computer, Windows 95 checks to see if a profile exists for that user locally or on the server, with the most recent version controlling. If a profile exists, then it's loaded into the Registry. If no profile exists, then Windows 95 will create a new profile using the default settings. When the user logs off, their profile will be updated to reflect any changes to the user settings.

> On Microsoft networks, user profiles are stored in the user's home directory if on the server. On NetWare networks, user profiles are stored in MAIL/user_ID.

You can create mandatory user profiles that force a user to use a preset array of settings. To do so, rename USER.DAT to USER.MAN. Although this mandatory profile may be edited in some situations (depending on what settings are in the user profile), those changes will not be added to the mandatory profile at user logoff.

> To enable user profiles, activate the Passwords applet in the Control Panel. On the User Profiles tab, choose the option that allows users to define a custom set of options that will be used when they log on.

File and Printer Sharing

User profiles offer no means of disabling file and printer sharing, but policies may, either on a per-user or per-computer basis. To disable file and printer sharing on a computer, you set up a system policy that disables sharing. To disable sharing for a specific user, you set up a user policy that restricts access to network settings and thus disables sharing.

Choosing a Workgroup or Domain

1. What Microsoft operating system should users choose if they are running Windows applications and need password protection of local files?

_____

2. True or False: You can install Windows 95 on an NT machine with NTFS partitions only.

3. What are the differences between long file name support in FAT partitions in Windows NT 3.5x and in Windows 95?

_____

4. Which network clients provide support for long file names? Choose all that apply.

A. MS Client for Microsoft Networks

B. MS Client for NetWare Networks

C. DOS Requester

D. NETX

5. List three Microsoft products to which the Client for Microsoft Networks can connect.

_____

_____

_____

6. True or False: Membership in a domain is required if you want to use user-level security in an all-Microsoft network.

7. The defining feature for a domain is that a Windows NT Server machine holds a(n) _____ for all the members of the domain.

8. How does using the domain security model simplify network administration for Microsoft networks?

_____

_____

_____

9. True or False: If a network includes Windows NT computers, it's a domain.

10. Would a workgroup model require users to be more or less network-savvy than a domain? Why?

_____

_____

Developing a Security Strategy

11.   List the three conditions that must exist to allow remote editing of the Registry on a PC.

_____

_____

_____

12.   Where does the Microsoft Client for NetWare Networks look for the CONFIG.POL file by default?

_____

13.   Where does the Client for MS Networks look for the CONFIG.POL file by default?

_____

14.   List the five custom folders supported with system policies.

_____

_____

_____

_____

_____

15. What happens with regard to remote administration when user-level security is installed?

_____

_____

_____

16. True or False: File and printer services need to be installed to use remote administration.

17. What is the mandatory profile file called?

_____

18. What are the two key differences between system policies and mandatory user profiles?

_____

_____

19. Which settings are loaded last, system policies or Registry settings?

_____

20. List the four folders and two files that make up a user profile.

_____

_____

_____

_____

_____

21. What system policy can you implement to ensure that a user cannot use the Run command from the Start menu?

_____

22. True or False: You can use system policies with real-mode clients.

23. What is the name and location of the default template file used by the System Policy Editor?

_____

24. True or False: Windows 95 supports merging changes to user profiles if a user is logged onto more than one PC.

25. True or False: System policies allow you to specify all computer and user settings.

26. When using the System Policy Editor, what are five policy categories for the Local User?

_____

_____

_____

_____

_____

27. True or False: System policies can be applied according to membership of existing groups on security providers (NetWare and NT Domain Servers).

28. True or False: If your computer is using share-level security, using NetWatcher, you can connect to other computers using user-level security.

29. _____ are always stored on a server, but

_____ may be stored either on a server or on the

local machine.

30. True or False: By default, when user profiles are enabled, all users will have the same Network Neighborhood settings.

31. If a user profile exists on both the server and on the workstation, which one controls if there are differences?

_____

32. To enable user profiles, you'd activate the _____

applet in the Control Panel.

33. True or False: Everyone who logs into a single Windows 95 workstation automatically logs into the same workgroup or domain.

34. Explain why system policies give you more detailed control over user settings than do mandatory user profiles.

_____

_____

_____

35. To disable password caching, you'd go to the _____
section of System Policies.

```
SAMPLE  TEST
```

1-1   What happens if a user who does not have a user profile logs onto a server when user profiles are enabled?

  A. The user will not be permitted to log on.

  B. A user profile will be created based on the default user profile and copied to the local computer.

  C. A user profile will be created based on the default user profile and copied to the network server.

  D. None of the above.

1-2   Where would you add names to the list of users entitled to remotely administer a machine?

  A. From the Passwords applet in the Control Panel, on the Remote Administration tab

  B. From the Passwords applet in the Control Panel, on the Users tab

  C. From the Remote Administration applet in the Control Panel, on the User tab

  D. None of the above

1-3   System policies:

  A. Can only be assigned to a user

  B. Can be assigned to a user or a group

  C. Can be assigned to a group, only if they are also assigned to one or more users

  D. None of the above

1-4 A roving user is logged onto the network from two different Windows 95 workstations. Changes are made to the user profile from both systems. Which of the following statements about the end result of the user profile are true after the user logs out of both connections?

    A. The user profile becomes a combination of both sets of changes.

    B. Both sets of changes are negated because the profile was open twice.

    C. The first set of changes to the profile are saved.

    D. The second set of changes to the profile are saved.

1-5 You want to maintain a user account database on a single server and use pass-through authentication. TCP/IP is the protocol of choice. Which of the following are valid choices for a network operating system on the login server?

    A. Windows NT

    B. NetWare

    C. Windows 95

    D. LAN Manager

1-6 You want to create a system policy that will prevent Jill from advertising her shared resources on a NetWare network, but make them available to the rest of the network. If Jill is using TCP/IP and IPX/SPX-compatible for her network protocols, which of the following settings should you disable?

    A. Disable SAP advertising

    B. Disable file sharing

    C. Disable Automatic NetWare login

    D. None of the above

1-7   Choose the setting or settings that can prevent Tonia from being able to change her password:

    A. Minimum Password Length

    B. Restrict Passwords Control Panel

    C. Restrict Network Control Panel

    D. Log Onto Windows NT

1-8   Choose the category within which you can disable file sharing for a computer.

    A. File and Printer Sharing for Microsoft Networks

    B. File and Printer Sharing for NetWare Networks

    C. Control Panel

    D. Sharing

1-9   To avoid the name of the last person logged on to appear in the logon dialog box, which Computer category should you select?

    A. Microsoft Client for Windows Networks

    B. Windows NT Logon

    C. Logon

    D. Password

1-10 System policies are downloaded to user computers based on:

    A. User name

    B. Computer name

    C. User ID

    D. Group ID

UNIT

2

Installation and Configuration

Test Objectives: Installation and Configuration

■ Install Windows 95. Installation options include:

- Automated Windows setup
- New
- Upgrade
- Uninstall
- Dual-boot combination with Windows NT

■ Install and configure the network components of a client computer and server in a Microsoft environment and a mixed Microsoft and NetWare environment.

■ Install and configure network protocols in a Microsoft environment and a mixed Microsoft and NetWare environment. Protocols include:

- NetBEUI
- IPX/SPX-compatible protocol
- TCP/IP
- Microsoft DLC
- PPTP/VPN

■ Install and configure hardware devices in a Microsoft environment and a mixed Microsoft and NetWare environment. Hardware devices include:

- Modems
- Printers

- Configure system services. Services include:
  - Browser

- Install and configure backup hardware and software. Hardware and software include:
  - Tape drives
  - The Backup application

NOTE Exam objectives are subject to change at any time without prior notice and at Microsoft's sole discretion. Please visit Microsoft's Training & Certification Web site (www.microsoft.com/Train_Cert/) for the most current listing of exam objectives.

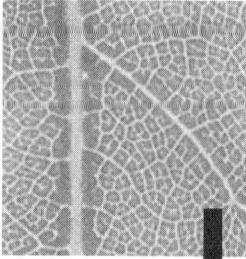

nstalling and configuring Windows 95 isn't a difficult task, but it can be a complex one. This chapter reviews methods of installing and configuring the basic components of Windows 95.

Installing Windows 95

nstalling Windows 95 can take several different forms:

- An automated installation, which may be a new installation or an upgrade, uses a predefined script to install the operating system with little or no user intervention.

- A new installation creates a new directory for the Windows 95 files, leaving any existing file systems intact.

- An upgrade overwrites settings for Windows 3.*x* (the only operating system upgradable to Windows 95) in the existing system directory.

- An uninstall option backs up your system files so you can uninstall Windows 95 components later.

- Dual-boot with Windows NT permits you to run both Windows 95 and Windows NT on the same computer, rebooting whenever you want to use the other operating system.

No matter what installation option you're using, some elements will be the same:

- The installation program is called SETUP.EXE, whether it's on floppy disks or CD-ROM.

- Setup may be run from either DOS or Windows but not from Windows NT.

- Except for device drivers required to run the network, CD-ROM, or hard disk, no terminate and stay resident (TSR) programs should be running during Setup.

- Virus-checking should be disabled in the computer's Setup program.

- The installation will consist of the following stages:

  - Information gathering (about the user and the computer)

  - Detecting the computer's hardware

  - Installing software components

  - Installing network components (where applicable)

  - Changing computer settings

  - Creating a Startup Disk

  - Copying files to the computer

Performing an Automatic Installation

Those installing Windows 95 on more than a few computers won't want to perform a manual installation for each. If your computers are networked, you have the option of creating an installation directory on a server and an installation script, then running the installation from there.

To run an automatic installation from the server, you'll need to run the server-based Setup program NETSETUP.EXE. This Setup program will create a basic installation script called MSBATCH.INF, which you can edit in a text editor such as Notepad.

Whereas Windows for Workgroups uses two different information files to configure various aspects of the operating system, Windows 95 relies mainly on MSBATCH.INF, a text file divided into sections corresponding to the various parts of the Setup process. With this information file, you can configure settings for:

- Customizing system settings

- Copying additional files or forcing Setup options

NOTE Windows and Windows for Workgroups used SETUP.SHH and SETUP.INI for settings comparable to those found in MSBATCH.INF.

Once you've created your version of MSBATCH.INF, you can incorporate it into an automated Setup by running Setup with the script*filename* option, where *filename* is the name you've assigned to the .INF file. (By default, it will be MSBATCH.INF, but you can rename it.) To install a variety of different options, just create more than one .INF file and choose the appropriate one.

You can run an automated Setup in one of three ways:

- As a logon script

- As a batch file

- Using server-based system administration software

> To initiate push installations from clients using protected-mode networking, create an entry in STARTUP.GRP to run Setup with a script file.

New Installation

To begin an installation into a new directory, move to the directory in which the installation program is located (this may be the floppy disk drive, the CD-ROM drive, or a network drive) and activate SETUP.EXE.

> If running Setup from within Windows, you can just find the file in the File Manager and double-click it.

In the course of the installation, you'll be prompted to pick a directory in which to install Windows 95. If a Windows directory already exists, you'll have the following choices:

- Install into the existing Windows directory (the default)

- Install into a new directory

To create a new installation, install into a new directory. Windows 95 will be installed without affecting any existing operating systems; you'll be able to boot into Windows if you choose.

> When installing into a new directory, you'll need to reinstall any Windows applications that were previously installed before they'll work with Windows 95.

When running Setup from the command line, you have access to a number of switches to let you customize the installation process:

/?	Provides help and lists the switches available for Setup.
/C	Runs Setup without loading the SmartDrive disk cache.
/d	Runs Setup without using the existing version of Windows (if any) during the early stages of installation. Use this option if Windows files are damaged or missing.
/id	Runs Setup without checking for the minimum free space required on the hard disk.
/ih	Runs ScanDisk in the foreground during Setup so that you can see the results. This switch is useful if you're experiencing hard disk errors.
/iL	Use this switch if you have a Logitech C mouse.
/iq	From DOS, runs Setup without running the ScanDisk quick check. Use this switch if you're using compression software other than DoubleSpace or DriveSpace.
/is	From Windows, runs Setup without running the ScanDisk quick check. Use this switch if you're using compression software other than DoubleSpace or DriveSpace.
/nostart	Copies a minimal installation of the Windows DLLs required by Windows 95 Setup, and then exits to DOS without installing Windows 95.
Script_file name	Specifies a file name for an unattended installation script.
/t:*tempdir*	Specifies a location to which temporary files will be copied during Setup. This directory must already exist, and any files already in it will be deleted.

Upgrading an Existing Installation

Upgrading an existing installation is similar to creating a new one, except for the directory into which you install. The upgrade, however, will preserve all settings from the previous installation of Windows (or Windows 95). All program groups, applications, and other settings will be migrated to Windows 95 so far as possible.

Uninstalling Windows 95

If you are running DOS 5 or later and upgrading from Windows 3.*x* or Windows for Workgroups, Setup will ask whether you want to back up your system files in preparation for uninstalling Windows 95. If you choose this option, then Setup will back up these files to the hard disk for possible future use.

To uninstall Windows 95, run the Add/Remove Programs applet in the Control Panel and move to the Install/Uninstall tab. Choose the components you want to remove.

Dual-Boot with Windows NT

Windows 95 and Windows NT can run on the same machine. So long as both operating systems are using the FAT file system, they can access the same hard disk partitions.

Windows NT has the option of two file systems (FAT and NTFS), but only FAT partitions are visible to local installations of Windows 95. However, NTFS partitions may be read via the network.

To set up Windows 95 on a system with Windows NT already installed, perform the following steps:

1. Make sure the Windows NT system is configured for dual-boot with DOS. To do so, edit BOOT.INI by adding

   BootMulti=1

2. Boot the Windows NT computer to DOS.

3. Run Windows 95 Setup as usual.

WARNING If you boot the Windows NT computer to DOS to run Windows 95 Setup, you will not be able to boot to Windows NT after DOS is completed. You'll need to use your Emergency Repair Disk to fix the damage.

To install Windows NT on a Windows 95 system, run winnt /w from Windows 95 to allow the Windows NT installation program to run under Windows. This switch will cause Setup to skip the reboot section of the Windows NT Setup.

Installing and Configuring Network Components

Some parts of your system may need to be installed and configured after the initial installation. In the Windows 95 world, network components are divided into four categories:

- Network protocols
- Network clients
- Network services
- Network adapters

All network components are added, removed, and configured via the same interface, the Configuration tab of the Network applet (see Figure 2.1).

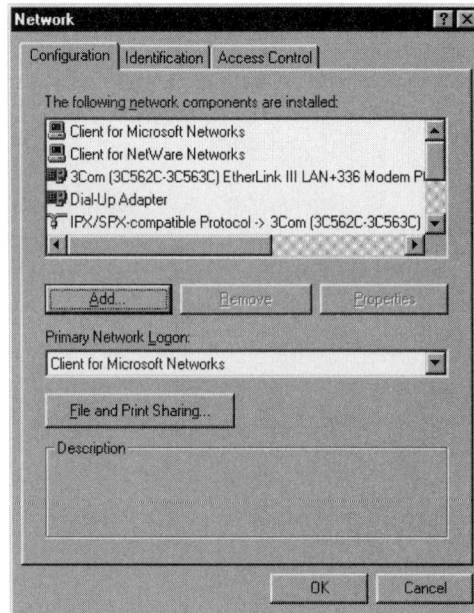

Network Protocols

A network protocol is a method of translating data into a form that can be transmitted across the network. For communication to take place between two computers, they must be using the same network protocol. Windows 95 supports the following protocols:

- NetBEUI
- TCP/IP
- IPX/SPX-compatible
- DLC
- PPTP

Each of these network protocols has its advantages and limitations. Net-BEUI is the fastest protocol, but it can only be used on all-Microsoft networks and is not routable. IPX/SPX-compatible is routable and is required for communication with NetWare networks. TCP/IP is the slowest of the main protocols. It is not available in a real-mode version so it won't work as the sole protocol for shared installations, but it is required for communication with the Internet and can be routed.

Each network protocol loaded uses system memory, so only load those protocols that you need. The protocols you need to install depend on both the network type and whether you're running a shared installation of Windows 95. Local installations may use only protected-mode clients, but shared installations must also run a real-mode protocol so they can connect to the Windows 95 server before the operating system is running.

To configure any of these protocols after installation, highlight the protocol's name in the list and click the Properties button, as described for Net-BEUI, TCP/IP, and IPX/SPX. If your computer has more than one network adapter installed, then one instance of the protocol will appear in the list of installed components for each adapter. Make sure that you're configuring the right one!

All transport protocols have different properties to configure, but you can set bindings for all of them—that is, you can configure which network hardware uses which protocol.

NetBEUI

NetBEUI comes preconfigured for the most part—it's even automatically installed if Windows 95 Setup detects it during installation. You can configure the settings that the protocol uses in real mode, however, such as those it would use when you boot in Safe Mode.

On the Advanced tab you can set real-mode values for NCBS and for Maximum Sessions (see Figure 2.2).

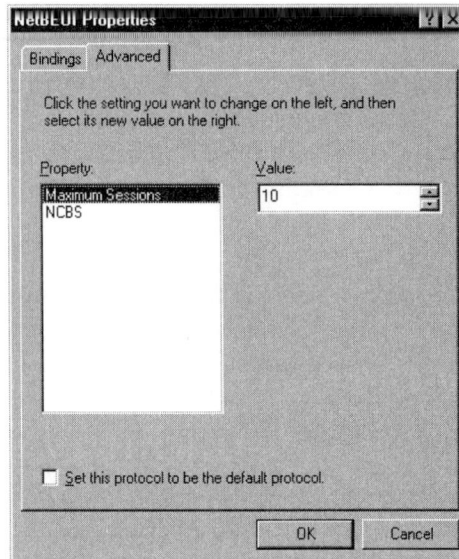

- NCBS (network control blocks) determines the number of NetBIOS commands that the protocol can use. The maximum is 18 (the total number of commands); the default is 12.

- Maximum Sessions identifies the maximum number of simultaneous connections (10 by default) that can be maintained to other computers via the redirector.

TCP/IP

TCP/IP has many more options to configure than does NetBEUI. In addition to bindings, you can configure:

- The IP address and subnet mask assigned to the adapter

- DNS

- WINS

- The gateway

IP Address and Subnet Mask Every host (computer or peripheral device directly attached to the network) on a TCP/IP network has an IP address that identifies it on the network. An IP address is a 32-bit binary number divided into four sections separated by dots and normally con-verted to decimal nomenclature so that it's easier to read. Some of these 32 bits identify the network, and some identify the host; the proportion of each depends on the network class (A, B, or C) and whether that network is subdivided.

If the network is divided into two or more physical sections and connected by routers—that is, *subnetted*—then each host is further identified, known both by its IP address and by its subnet. Subnet location is identified by a set of numbers called the *subnet mask*. This is another 32-bit binary number assigned to each section of network. To conform to the subnet mask, an IP address must match all the placement of 1s in the networking part of the address. The default subnet mask is 255.255.255.255, which is all binary 1s.

By default, Windows 95 assumes that you'll be using a DHCP (Dynamic Host Configuration Protocol) server to automatically assign IP addresses from its available pool. If you know that you have a fixed IP address, click Specify an IP Address and enter the address and the subnet mask (see Figure 2.3).

FIGURE 2.3

Let DHCP assign an IP address to you or choose it yourself.

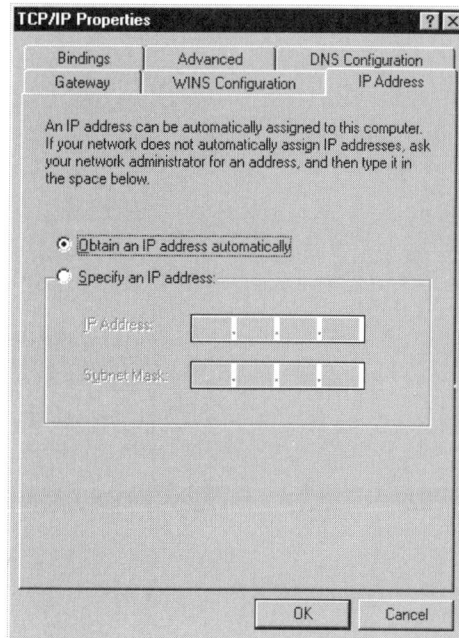

DNS Configuration IP addresses are all very well for computers, but humans find it easier to remember joe.company.com than 10101101 11100110 11011011 10011011 or even 173.230.219.155. Converting the names that people can remember to IP addresses that machines can use is called *name resolution*; Windows NT comes with two forms of name resolution that you can use:

DNS The Domain Naming Service resolves host names.

WINS The Windows Internet Naming Service resolves NetBIOS names.

With this name resolution, each address user can use the form most comfortable for them.

Not all networks use DNS (although you are if you're connected to the Internet). Setup for DNS support from Windows 95 is accomplished from the DNS Configuration tab (see Figure 2.4).

FIGURE 2.4

Identify your DNS servers.

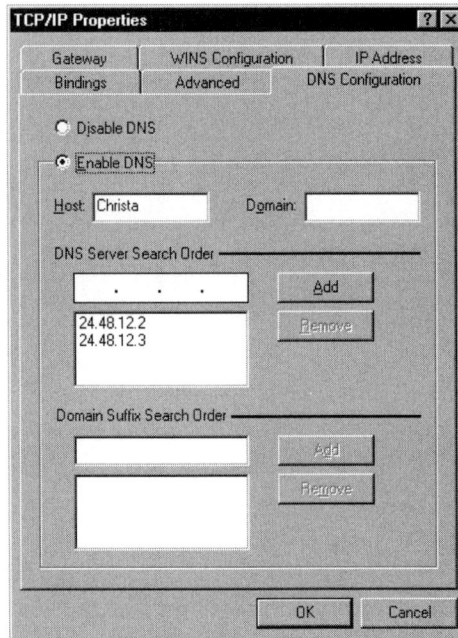

- **Host** should be the name of the local computer or user. It's combined with the domain name or suffix to make a fully qualified domain name.

Fully qualified domain names (FQDN) and e-mail addresses are not the same thing. If your host name is Maria and your domain centers.com, then your FQDN would be maria.centers.com, not Maria@centers.com. Maria's e-mail address could be something entirely different, such as Fuzzy@centers.com.

- **Domain** is not the name of the Windows NT domain (if any) but of the company domain if there is one.

- **DNS Server Search Order** lists the DNS servers available (two are often provided for redundancy). The DNS server maintains a static list of name-to-address mappings. If one DNS server does not respond, then the second one is queried. However, if the first does not have a listing for the name or address, then the second one is not queried— the second one comes into play *only* if the first is unavailable.

To change the search order of DNS servers, delete the first one and re-add it; DNS servers are searched in the order in which they're added.

- **Domain Suffix Search Order** provides a place for you to supply a domain to identify your computer on the Internet.

WINS Configuration   DNS resolves host names and IP addresses. To resolve NetBIOS names (the 16-character names used to identify computers on the network), you'll need a WINS server. WINS servers are distinct from DNS servers not only in terms of the names they resolve, but in how they do it: Just as DNS servers maintain static lists of name and address mappings that must be manually updated, WINS servers maintain and update their databases dynamically.

To configure WINS use with Windows 95, turn to the WINS Configuration tab in the TCP/IP Properties dialog box (see Figure 2.5).

F I G U R E 2.5

Identify WINS servers.

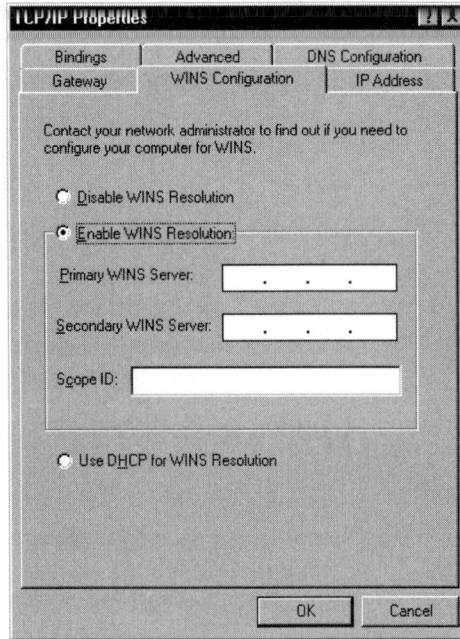

F I G U R E 2.5

Identify WINS servers.

- **Enable/Disable WINS Resolution** turns access to the WINS servers on and off, once it's been made available once. By default, it's off.

- **Primary WINS Server** and **Secondary WINS Server** are the IP addresses of the WINS server(s). If there's more than one, then they should have the same information.

- **Scope ID** identifies a group of computers that recognize a certain NetBIOS name. Computers with the same Scope ID will be able to hear each other's broadcast messages.

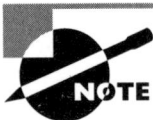

> **NOTE** If you've chosen to let a DHCP server supply you with an IP address, then the DHCP server will supply you with WINS information.

Gateway   Gateways are links between subnets. On the Gateway tab you supply the name of the gateway(s) to use (see Figure 2.6).

FIGURE 2.6

Add gateway IP addresses in the order in which they should be searched.

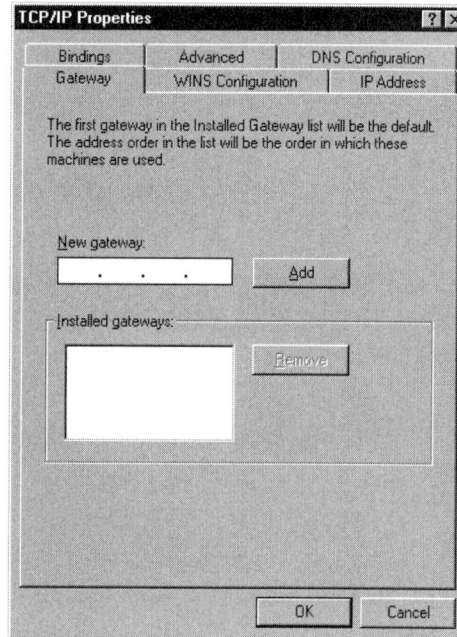

FIGURE 2.6

Add gateway IP addresses in the order in which they should be searched.

> Like DNS servers, gateways will be tried in the order added, but in this case, they'll be tried until one works.

To add a new gateway, type its IP address in the list and click the Add button. To remove one, highlight it in the list and click the Remove button.

IPX/SPX-Compatible

Most of the options used to configure IPX/SPX-compatible protocols have to do with frame type. Most of these are automatically configured and shouldn't require edits, but if you need to adjust them you can turn to the Advanced tab of the Properties dialog box (see Figure 2.7).

These settings are described in Table 2.1.

F I G U R E 2.7

Setting frame type
options

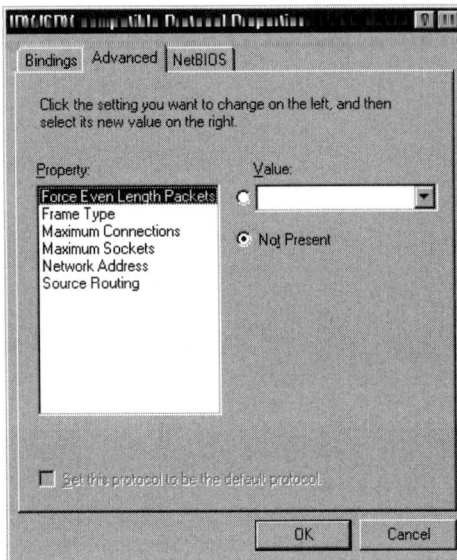

T A B L E 2.1: IPX/SPX-Compatible Advanced Configuration Options

Property	Description	Default Value When Present
Force Even-Length Packets	Causes all packets to be of even length. Used only by Ethernet 802.3 monolithic implementations that cannot handle odd-length packets	No
Frame Type	Specifies the frame type to be used by network adapters that can handle different frame types. Normally, when the computer joins the network Windows 95 determines the prevalent frame type by sending a RIP request and examining the returned frame types, choosing the most common as the default frame type	Auto
Maximum Connections	Specifies the maximum number of connections that IPX will allow	1
Maximum Sockets	Specifies the maximum number of sockets that IPX assigns	2

T A B L E 2.1: IPX/SPX-Compatible Advanced Configuration Options *(continued)*

Property	Description	Default Value When Present
Network Address	A 32-bit value that identifies the network address	NA
Source Routing	Used on Token Ring networks to determine the number of entries that should be permitted in the cache	16-count, if in use

> **NOTE** On the Bindings tab, IPX/SPX will always be bound to the Microsoft Client for NetWare. This client cannot be bound to another protocol.

The latter two network protocols are less often used than the first three. DLC is only used in very specific circumstances: to connect to IBM mainframes or to connect to network printers not connected to a print server. PPTP (Point to Point Tunneling Protocol), available in beta for Windows 95, may be used to create virtual private networks, connecting to corporate networks via a Dial-up Networking connection.

Network Clients

Windows 95 supports two Microsoft network clients out of the box:

- The Client for Microsoft Networks, used for all Microsoft network types (LAN Manager, Windows NT, Windows 95 networks, and so forth)

- The Client for NetWare Networks, used for connecting to NetWare servers

> **NOTE** The Novell Workstation shell cannot be installed in conjunction with the Client for NetWare Networks.

Windows 95 also comes with drivers for connecting to Banyan and Sun-Soft networks, as well as an NFS connector and NetWare drivers.

To install a client, open the Network applet in the Control Panel and move to the Configuration tab. Click on the Add button, and select Clients from the list of available component types. In some cases, such as for the NFS client, you may be prompted for a manufacturer's disk, but otherwise the client will be installed without further action on your part.

The properties available for each client vary (or none may be available), but they generally show how to connect to the servers on the chosen network. Figure 2.8 shows the Properties boxes available for the Client for Microsoft Networks and the Client for NetWare Networks.

FIGURE 2.8

Configuring the clients for Microsoft and NetWare networks

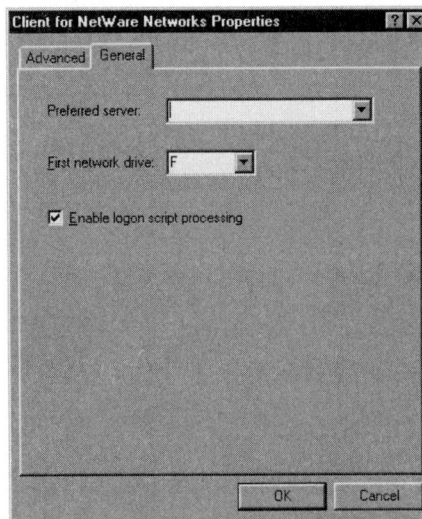

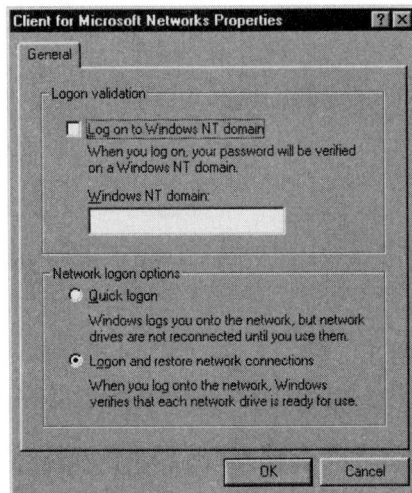

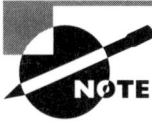

> You cannot run both real-mode and protected-mode clients on shared installations of Windows 95.

Network Services

The Browser service permits that computer to maintain a copy of the browse list, a list of all network resources. On Microsoft networks, a computer called the *master browser* maintains the main browse list, and other computers called *backup browsers* maintain copies of this browse list so that not all the computers in the network have to query the master browser to view network resources.

To enable and configure the Browser service, move the Configuration tab in the Network applet in the Control Panel. Install file and printer sharing if it's not already installed, and click on its Properties button.

Set the value of the Browse Master property to Automatic (the default), Disabled, or Enabled (see Figure 2.9).

FIGURE 2.9

Setting up the Browser service

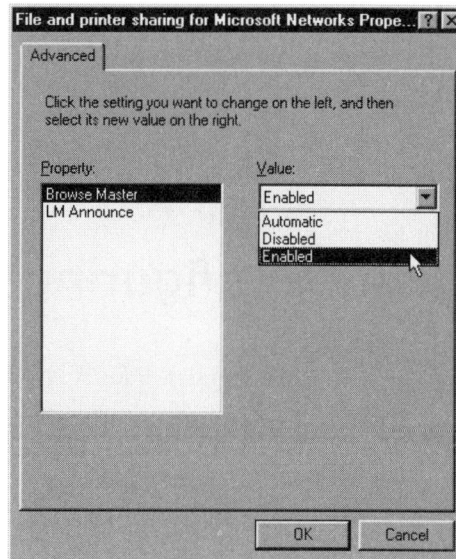

What are the results of these settings?

- Setting Browse Master to Automatic will permit the computer to become a master or backup browser if necessary.

- Setting Browse Master to Disabled will prevent this computer from maintaining a browse list at all.

- Setting Browse Master to Enabled will make the computer the master browser for the workgroup.

> **NOTE** Microsoft recommends a ratio of about 15 workstations to each backup browser.

Network Adapters

Network adapters may also be installed via the Configuration tab. Once again, click the Add button, choose to install an adapter, and choose the correct make and model available from the list. If you have a manufacturer's disk for your adapter, click the Have Disk button.

Network adapters may be configured according to whether their drivers operate in real mode or protected mode and according to the network protocols bound to them. (If they're protected mode to begin with; real-mode drivers don't have this flexibility.) You can run one network protocol on one network adapter but not another, if you wish.

Installing and Configuring Hardware

When you first boot Windows 95 after attaching a new device, in most cases the device will be detected automatically. Plug-and-Play (PnP) devices, such as PC-Card modems, will be detected and automatically configured. Other devices will be configured, but you'll have to use the appropriate wizard to set them up.

Installing and Configuring a Modem

You can start the process of installing a modem in one of three ways:

- Running a communications program
- Activating the Modems applet in the Control Panel
- Running the Add New Hardware Wizard in the Control Panel

Whichever method you use, the Install New Modem Wizard appears, asking you whether you want Windows 95 to detect the modem (by default, it will) or you want to specify it yourself. From here, answer the questions put to you and the proper drivers will be installed.

> **TIP**
>
> If Windows 95 doesn't detect the modem, it may not be properly connected or there may be a resource conflict.

This procedure may vary slightly in a couple of circumstances:

- If you're installing a legacy internal modem, you'll need to configure the COM port to which you want to connect the modem. In most cases, the Add New Modem Wizard will take care of this, but in some cases you must run the Add New Hardware Wizard.
- PC-Card modems are automatically detected on system boot and the proper drivers are installed.

Installing and Configuring a Printer

To install a new printer, activate the Add Printer Wizard found in the Printers folder. This wizard works like the Add New Hardware Wizard except it will not automatically detect your printer; you must specify the make and model of the printer.

To set up a local printer, you'll:

- Specify the make and model of the printer.
- Choose a port to which to connect (or specify that it will print to a file).
- Name the printer.
- Copy the appropriate driver files to the computer.

You can't install two devices at once, so you cannot run the Add New Hard ware Wizard and the Add Printer Wizard at the same time.

To configure a printer after it's already installed, open the Printers folder, right-click on the printer to be configured, and choose Properties from the pop-up menu that appears. To configure most printer properties, you'll need to move to the Details tab (see Figure 2.10).

FIGURE 2.10

Configuring a printer

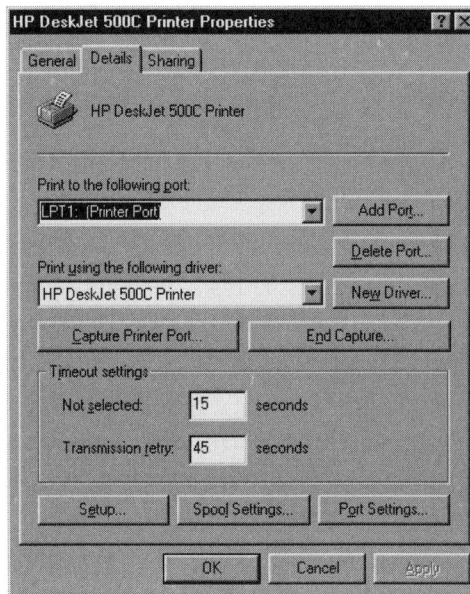

A printer's Properties dialog box has two tabs: one for a general description of the printer and one for more detailed configuration information. When the printer is shared with the network, a third (as shown in Figure 2.10) is added: Sharing.

Installing and Configuring Backup Hardware and Software

Backing up is crucial, and to make the job easier, Windows 95 includes backup software. This software is not installed by default, so you'll have to configure both it and the backup hardware you choose.

Setting Up a Tape Drive

Installing a tape drive is like installing other hardware. Run the Add New Hardware Wizard, let Windows 95 detect your tape drive, choose the proper driver, and the hardware will be installed.

> **NOTE** Windows 95 supports only two categories of QIC 40, 80, and 3010 backup devices: those connecting to the floppy controller and those connecting to a parallel port. For a list of manufacturers, check Backup Help.

Setting Up Backup for Windows 95

To install Backup, activate the Add/Remove Programs applet in the Control Panel and move to the Windows Setup tab. Select Disk Tools from the list and click the Details button (see Figure 2.11).

> **NOTE** To install Backup, you'll need access to the Windows 95 installation files, whether on disks, CD-ROM, or your server.

Once Backup is installed, you can locate it in the System Tools section of the Accessories folder. By default, Windows 95 Backup will do a full system backup, copying all files (including Registry files).

To configure Backup, choose Options from the Settings menu. From the dialog box that appears, you'll be able to configure the backup, restore, and file-comparison processes.

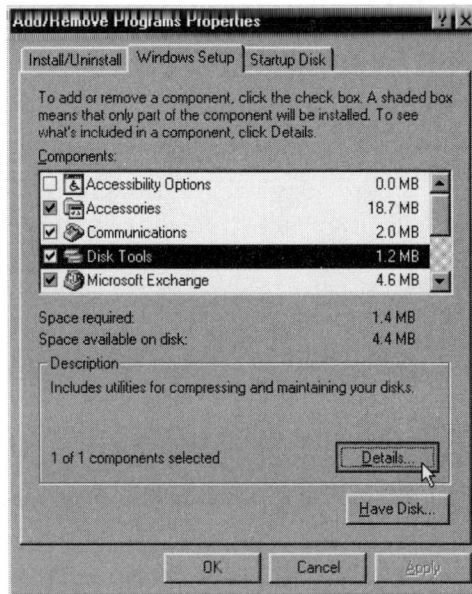

You can create backup sets and save them to back up only certain parts of your hard disk—for example, backing up only your data directories instead of application directories.

Installing Windows 95

1. True or False: You can dual-boot Windows 95 and DR/Novell DOS.

2. The _____ utility has an option to create a default script and the MSBATCH.INF file for setting up the workstations from a shared network installation.

3. What setting must be present in MSDOS.SYS to enable dual-boot?

_____

4. If Windows 3.1 is currently installed on a computer and you choose to install Windows 95 to the same directory, the configuration settings from which three .INI files will be moved to the Windows 95 Registry?

_____

_____

_____

5. How do you convert .GRP files to Windows 95's new folders and links?

_____

6. What must you do to keep your Windows 3.x settings when upgrading to Windows 95?

_____

7. True or False: You can run Windows 95 Setup from DOS.

8. True or False: If you install Windows 95 into your existing Windows directory, you will need to reinstall applications.

9. What are the four Setup types that Windows 95 Setup offers?

_____

_____

_____

_____

10. What .INF file allows for automated running of Windows 95 Setup?

_____

11. What file must you create to restrict a user's choice of Workgroups to join when running Setup?

_____

12. True or False: You can dual-boot Windows 95 and OS/2.

13. True or False: You can dual-boot Windows 95 and Windows NT.

14. What is the minimum amount of conventional memory required by the Windows 95 Setup routine?

_____

15. List the three predefined Computer Roles that can be used to optimize file system performance.

_____

_____

_____

16. True or False: The floppy version of Windows 95 does not have all the files available on the CD version.

17. List the three key advantages of a shared Windows 95 installation.

_____

_____

_____

18. Windows 95 allows you to boot from a local hard disk to run a shared installation. Alternately, you can also boot from a(n) _____ or a computer with a(n) _____ to run the shared installation.

19. The _____ file records the results of Network card/component detection.

20. Your computer is set up to dual-boot between MS-DOS and Windows 95. You see files with the .W40 and .DOS extensions in your root directory. What are these files?

_____

21. Windows 3.*x* used .SHH files to store information for an automated Setup. Under Windows 95, which file would you create and modify to store the same settings?

_____

22. True or False: You can install Windows 95 on a PC running MS DOS 3.1.

23. Can you set up and install DOS to allow dual-boot after Windows 95 has been installed? What versions of DOS will this work with?

_____

24. True or False: You need to run Setup on each computer on which you want to run a shared installation of Windows 95.

25. True or False: You can install a local copy of Windows 95 onto a machine with a 40MB hard disk.

26. True or False: You can install Windows 95 on an NT machine that has a FAT partition.

27. True or False: The long file name support for FAT partitions in NT 3.5x is compatible with that of Windows 95.

28. From the Server-Based Setup dialog box, what option would you choose to edit the MSBATCH.INF file?

_____

29. The Briefcase utility is only installed by default when running the _____ Setup type.

30. During an upgrade of a Windows 3.1 workstation to Windows 95, .GRP files are converted to subdirectories of which directory?

_____

31. The _____ switch can be used with the SETUP.EXE program to prevent Windows 95 from checking the minimum disk space requirements during installation.

32. The _____ switch can be used with the SETUP.EXE program when it is being run from DOS to prevent ScanDisk from running during the installation.

33. Which Setup type would you use for workstations that have limited disk space available?

_____

34. What installation type do you need to select to be given the option of selecting network components?

_____

35. True or False: Windows 95 Setup will allow you to format a hard disk during installation.

36. List the three key advantages of a local installation of Windows 95.

_____

_____

_____

37. Windows 95 will support a maximum of _____ network adapters in a single computer.

38. What does the NETDET.INI file control?

_____

39. True or False: Windows 95 can be installed on a computer that has only an HPFS partition.

40. Under a shared installation, which file contains a listing of the machine directory and drive letters to be connected to for each client?

_____

41. What is meant by a "push installation"?

_____

42. How do you initiate push installations from clients using protected-mode networking?

_____

_____

43. True or False: A server-based Setup can only be created from a computer running Windows 95.

44. When creating a shared installation, a minimum of _____ MB of disk space is required on the server.

45. During installation, what is AUTOEXEC.BAT renamed to?

_____

46. A(n) _____ installation leaves existing file systems intact.

47. List the PC-compatible operating systems from which Windows 95 Setup cannot be run.

_____

48. Your hard disk is compressed with Stacker. Which switch should you use with SETUP.EXE, and what will this switch do?

_____

_____

49. True or False: To uninstall Windows 95, you must be running DOS 3.3 or later and upgrading from either Windows or Windows for Workgroups.

Installing and Configuring Network Components

50. Under the TCP/IP Properties dialog box, which tab must you select to review what services will be able to make use of TCP/IP?

_____

51. List the three main transport protocols that ship with Windows 95.

_____

_____

_____

52. How would you configure an Intel network adapter for use with Windows 95?

_____

53. How many master browsers can there be on a Windows 95 MS Net Workgroup?

_____

54. How many protected-mode network components can you install in Windows 95?

_____

55. On a peer-to-peer network, a Windows 95 station will be chosen as the Browse Master instead of a WFWG station because of a(n) _____ of the browsing software.

56. True or False: Windows 95 fully supports older NDIS2 and ODI network drivers by use of mappers (or shims) that emulate NDIS 3.1 drivers.

57. True or False: You can run Microsoft's protected-mode clients on top of real-mode drivers such as ODI on shared installations.

58. True or False: You can use shared network installations on a TCP/IP-only network.

59. When installing legacy devices, you will need to run the Add New Hardware Wizard. What must you run when installing Plug-and-Play devices?

_____

60. To use Microsoft's protected-mode clients on a shared network installation, what sort of drivers do you need for the network card?

_____

61. What drivers can you use to load shared network copies of Windows 95?

_____

62. What tool do you use to configure transport protocols?

_____

63. If NetBEUI is your only transport protocol, by default you can establish up to _____ simultaneous connections.

64. True or False: A subnetted network will not use the default subnet mask.

65. True or False: If you're using a DHCP server to lease IP addresses on your network, you won't need to specify a subnet mask.

66. Explain how a subnet mask identifies to which subnet an IP address belongs.

_____

_____

_____

67. True or False: DNS may only be used in a network with a primary domain controller, as DNS requires a domain name to operate.

68. How is DNS search order determined?

_____

69. Whereas DNS servers maintain _____ mappings of names to IP addresses, WINS servers maintain a(n) _____ set of mappings.

70. True or False: A Scope ID identifies the set of IP addresses that a DHCP server makes available for a single subnet.

71. How does DNS search precedence differ from gateway search precedence?

_____

_____

_____

72. The Microsoft Client for NetWare Networks will always be bound to

_____.

73. You don't want a particular Windows 95 machine to become a master browser. This machine is part of a mixed Windows NT-Windows 95 network with about a hundred nodes, and all Windows NT machines are available as browsers. Do you need to change the default settings for the Browse Master service? Why or why not?

_____

_____

_____

Installing and Configuring Hardware

74. Instead of spooling raw printer data, Windows 95 uses the _____ format for improved performance.

75. True or False: Windows 95 will automatically detect and install Plug-and-Play (PnP) devices provided your computer has a PnP BIOS.

76. After Windows 95 is installed, you can have it detect and install new drivers for network cards by selecting the _____ option under Control Panel.

77. True or False: You can manually override resource settings for devices with Device Manager.

78. How should you tell Windows 95 that you have added/are about to add new hardware?

_____

79. How would you specify a new device driver for a device?

_____

80. If you change resource settings for non-PnP devices in Device Manager, what else should you do to make sure the devices work?

_____

81. True or False: Plug-and-Play cards are available for the EISA bus design, but not for the ISA bus.

STUDY QUESTIONS

82. What tool do you use to configure the COM port settings in TAPI-enabled applications?

_____

83. Bill is using three different Windows 95–based communications packages. How many times must he install and configure the modem?

_____

84. True or False: The Modem Installation Wizard will attempt to detect the type of modem you have.

Installing and Configuring Backup Hardware and Software

85. Windows 95's Backup supports two backup types: _____
and _____.

86. True or False: You can only back up to either floppy drives or tape drives.

87. What's a simple way of running the same backup operation over and over again?

_____

_____

2-1 You're scanning the files in Explorer, trying to find the one that holds information about how your modem is configured. What files specify device configuration information?

    A. .POL files

    B. .CON files

    C. .INF files

    D. All of the above

2-2 Typically, how many computers must exist in a Windows 95 MS Net Workgroup before a backup browse server is needed?

    A. 10

    B. 30

    C. 20

    D. 15

2-3 What command must be included in the MSDOS.SYS file to enable dual-boot in Windows 95?

    A. MultiBoot=1

    B. DoubleBoot=2

    C. Boot=0

    D. BootMulti=1

2-4 How do you specify a network card boot PROM installation of Windows 95?

    A. Add the command RBPSetup=1 to the [Network] section of the MSBATCH.INF file.

    B. Add the command RPLSetup=1 to the [Network] section of the MSBATCH.INF file.

    C. Run Setup with the /RPL switch.

    D. Add the command RPLSetup=1 to the [Location] section of the MSBATCH.INF file.

2-5   What sort of program is Windows 95 Setup?

    A. A 16-bit, protected-mode application

    B. A 32-bit, protected-mode application

    C. A batch file that runs WIN.COM with the /I switch

    D. None of the above

2-6   Choose all that apply. The machine directory:

    A. Contains files specific to a user

    B. Contains files specific to a computer

    C. Includes the full registry

    D. Stores the information in HKEY_DYN_DATA

2-7   How do you set up a shared network installation of Windows 95?

    A. Run SETUP.EXE /a

    B. Run SETUP.EXE /n

    C. Run INSTALL.EXE

    D. Run NETSETUP.EXE

2-8   You need to specify a network number for the IPX/SPX protocol to use when:

    A. You would like the workstation to access servers across a router.

    B. You would like the workstation to use SAP.

    C. You would like to install two network cards in the workstation and use Windows 95 internal routing features.

    D. Never.

2-9 How many network clients can you install in Windows 95?

   A. One real-mode and multiple protected-mode clients

   B. Two real-modes and one protected-mode client

   C. One real-mode and no protected-mode clients

   D. Multiple protected-mode clients and multiple real-mode clients

2-10 What part of Windows 95 should you use to install modems?

   A. The Modem Installation Wizard

   B. The Communications Installation Wizard

   C. Explorer

   D. The Setup utility

2-11 What is the recommended method to configure resource settings for hardware devices?

   A. From the Device Manager tab of the System Properties dialog box

   B. By using REGEDIT

   C. By using POLEDIT

   D. From the Hardware Profiles tab of the System Properties dialog box

2-12 Within the Registry, ISA configuration options for non-PnP adapters are stored:

   A. Dynamically

   B. Statically

   C. Neither A nor B

   D. A and B

2-13   Which two components comprise the NDIS 2 to NDIS 3.1 mapper?

    A. NDIS2SUP.VXD

    B. NDIS3SUP.VXD

    C. NDISHELP.SYS

    D. NDISHLP.SYS

2-14   The fundamental difference between WINS and DNS is:

    A. WINS applies only to the local network.

    B. WINS applies to NetBIOS names, and DNS to host names

    C. WINS information is not routable.

    D. None of the above.

2-15   To map the name server.com to an IP address, what do you need?

    A. A WINS server

    B. A DHCP server

    C. A DNS server

    D. A gateway

2-16   The NCBS setting controls:

    A. The number of NetBIOS commands available to NetBEUI

    B. The protocol used to identify routers on a TCP/IP network

    C. Whether NetWare servers are visible in a TCP/IP network

    D. The frame size for NetBEUI networks

2-17 According to Microsoft, at which point do you need a backup browser?

    A. Always

    B. When the number of nodes in the network exceeds 30

    C. When the primary domain controller is bogged down by user logons

    D. None of the above

2-18 Which configurable property do all network protocols have in common?

    A. SMBs

    B. Packet type

    C. Source routing

    D. Bindings

UNIT

3

Configuring and
Managing Resource Access

Test Objectives: Configuring and Managing Resource Access

- Assign access permissions for shared folders in a Microsoft environment and a mixed Microsoft and NetWare environment. Methods include:
  - Passwords
  - User permissions
  - Group permissions

- Create, share, and monitor resources. Resources include:
  - Remote
  - Network printers
  - Shared fax modem
  - Unimodem/V

- Set up user environments by using user profiles and system policies.

- Back up data and restore data.

- Manage hard disks. Tasks include:
  - Disk compression
  - Partitioning

- Establish application environments for Microsoft MS-DOS applications.

NOTE Exam objectives are subject to change at any time without prior notice and at Microsoft's sole discretion. Please visit Microsoft's Training and Certification Web site (www.microsoft.com/Train_Cert/) for the most current listing of exam objectives.

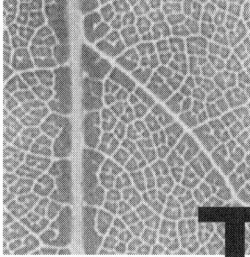

The following sections review methods of sharing resources with networks and protecting those resources from data loss and user tampering. This chapter also discusses some elements of disk management.

Setting Access Permissions for Shared Folders

By default, resources shared with the rest of the network are not protected. Anyone who can see them also has full access to them. Network shares can be protected using any of three methods:

- Passwords
- User permissions
- Group permissions

The latter two are pretty much the same; the main distinction between user and group permissions is that user permissions are based on who you are (account name) and group permissions are based on what you know (password).

> **TIP**
>
> You must enable File and Print Sharing services before you can share a resource.

Setting Up Passwords

To set up a password for a shared folder, select the folder, right-click on it, and choose Properties (or Sharing—they both work) from the pop-up menu that appears. In the Sharing tab shown in Figure 3.1, choose an access type and enter a password. Access types are described in Table 3.1.

FIGURE 3.1

Setting the password for a shared folder

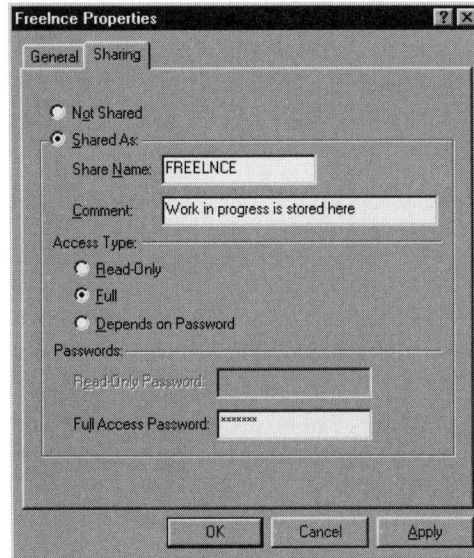

To set passwords for individual shares, you must be in share-level security mode, the default in Windows 95. You can specify share-level security in the Access Control tab of the Network Control Panel.

TABLE 3.1	**Defined Access Type**	**Description**
Folder Access Types	Read-Only	Shares the folder so other people can read its contents, but not change or delete them
	Full Control	Shares the folder so other people can read or change the folder's contents

T A B L E 3.1 *(cont.)*	**Defined Access Type**	**Description**
Folder Access Types	Depends on Password	Sets a different password for each type of access. You must set a password for at least one access type, as the two passwords must be different

Setting Up User and Group Permissions

Windows 95 does not have its own user-level permissions set up. Instead, it uses pass-through security to authenticate user requests. These requests are then sent to the Windows NT or NetWare computer specified on the Windows 95 machine and compared against the entries in the server accounts database.

To set up user-level permissions, go to the Access Control tab of the Network Control Panel and specify User-Level Access Control (see Figure 3.2). Then, type in the name of the computer (for NetWare networks) or domain (for Windows NT networks) storing the user accounts database.

F I G U R E 3.2

To use user-level access control, you must specify a server to provide pass-through authentication.

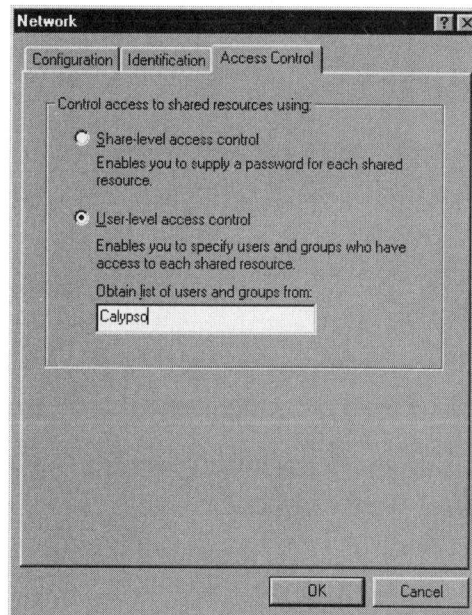

Group permissions and user permissions work pretty much the same way, determining access depending on the rights and permissions assigned either to an individual or to a group.

Creating, Sharing, and Monitoring Network Resources

You can share resources other than files with the network. You can create and protect shares for printers and fax modems and provide remote access to the network via a Windows 95 machine.

Windows 95 supports the Universal Naming Convention (UNC), which allows you to map network shares for folders and printers without assigning a drive letter. The syntax for UNC is as follows: *servername**folder* or *servername**printer*, where:

- *servername* is the name of the server

- *folder* is the name of the shared directory

- *printer* is the name of the shared printer

If you know a resource's UNC name, you can map it directly with Network Neighborhood's Map Network Drive option.

Remote Access

Depending on the setup, you may need to configure a Windows 95 machine so someone can connect to another system or dial into that system, or possibly both.

Configuring a Windows 95 Computer for Dial-up Connection

To make a new connection to dial into a computer, follow these steps:

1. In the Dial-up Networking folder in My Computer, right-click the Make New Connection icon and choose Create from the pop-up menu.

2. Follow the wizard that appears, naming the connection, choosing a modem type, and providing a number.

3. When the new connection is created, right-click on its icon in the DUN folder and choose Properties from the pop-up menu.

4. In General Properties, click on the Server Type button (see Figure 3.3).

FIGURE 3.3

Configuring a dial-up connection

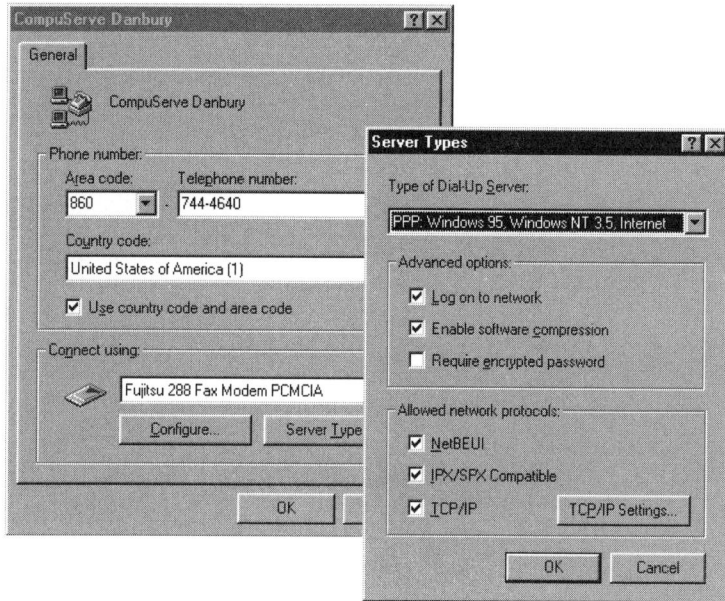

5. Choose the appropriate server type and protocol (see Table 3.2).

6. Select the appropriate logon, password, and compression option.

7. Click OK to apply the settings.

TABLE 3.2

Dial-up Connection Types

Server Type	Connection Type
PPP, Windows NT 3.5 or later, Windows 95, Internet	Default option, detecting and connecting to remote access servers running TCP/IP, NetBEUI, or IPX/SPX over PPP
NetWare Connect	NetWare Connect running IPX/SPX

T A B L E 3.2 *(cont.)*	Server Type	Connection Type
Dial-up Connection Types	Windows for Workgroups and Windows NT 3.1	Windows 95 server, Windows NT 3.1 or 3.5, Windows for Workgroups using NetBEUI over RAS
	SLIP: Unix Connection	Any SLIP server over TCP/IP
	CSLIP: Unix Connection	Any SLIP server over TCP/IP that uses header compression

NOTE SLIP is not automatically installed with Windows 95. To use the SLIP protocol, you must install it from the Windows 95 CD.

Configuring a Windows 95 Computer to Be a Dial-up Server

If you have the Dial-up Server component of Microsoft Plus installed, you can configure a Windows 95 computer to be a dial-up server. This connection will support a single user connecting with NetBEUI or the IPX/SPX-compatible protocol.

Windows 95's Dial-up Server does not allow access to the entire network, but to the machine to which you're dialing. For full network access, you'll need to dial into a computer running a fuller remote-access service, such as one using Windows NT's RAS or NetWare's NetConnect.

Network Printers

To share a printer with the network, follow these steps:

1. In the Printers folder, right-click the printer to be shared and choose Sharing from the pop-up menu.

2. On the Sharing tab that appears, select the Shared As option (see Figure 3.4).

3. Give the printer a name, and a description and password if desired.

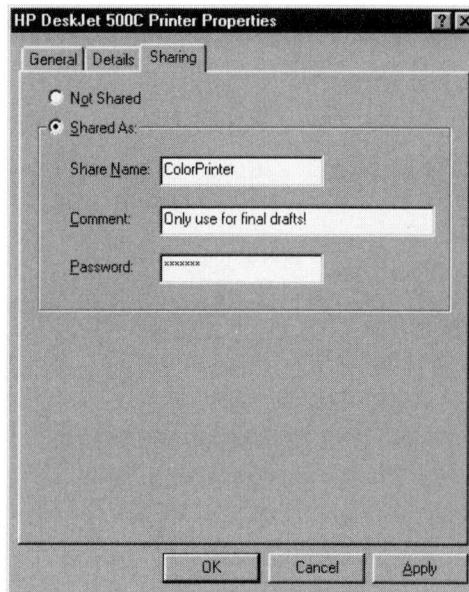

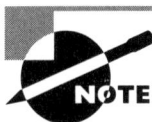

To share a printer with the network, you must have the file and printer service installed. To make a printer available to NetWare computers, you must
install MSPSRV.

You can monitor the print jobs spooled to a printer and see who's sending
them by double-clicking on the job's icon in the Printers folder. The print
job, its size, its status, and its sender are all displayed. You can delete or
pause these print jobs from this window.

Shared Fax Modem

With Microsoft Fax installed, you can share a fax modem on one Windows 95
machine with the rest of the network. Faxes will come into the fax server, go
into its Exchange mailbox, and then get routed to the mailboxes of the
intended recipients.

To make a computer a fax server with MS Fax, follow these steps:

1. In Microsoft Exchange, choose Tools ➤ Microsoft Fax Tools ➤ Options.

2. Move to the Modems tab in the Microsoft Fax Properties dialog box.

3. Make sure that the option to allow others to use your modem to send faxes is checked.

4. Set up fax security:

   ▪ If you have user-level security enabled, list those who are eligible to use the fax modem.

   ▪ If you have share-level security enabled, choose a password for the fax modem and dispense it.

   ▪ If you choose Full Access, then all users on the network can send faxes. This is the default option.

> **NOTE** Windows 95 comes with Unimodem V, the latest generation of universal voice/fax/data modem drivers. Most of the software required to make the modem operate under Windows 95 is in this driver; manufacturers have only to write a simple driver called a *minidriver* to make their devices function under Windows 95. Most of Windows 95's drivers follow the universal driver/minidriver paradigm.

Microsoft recommends the minimum configuration for a fax server be a 486-based computer with 12MB of RAM running as a non-dedicated fax server. The modem in use should transmit at least 14.4Kbps.

Setting Up System Policies and User Profiles

Use system policies or user profiles to customize the operating environment on a machine or for a particular user. System policies can affect both user-specific and computer-specific settings, whereas user profiles affect only user settings.

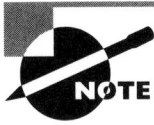

> **NOTE** Whether you're using system policies or user profiles, or a combination of both, you must enable user profiles from the Passwords applet in the Control Panel.

As shown in Table 3.3, user profiles and system policies are each implemented differently.

T A B L E 3.3: User Profiles

	User Profiles	System Policies
File Name	USER.DAT	CONFIG.POL
Location	May be stored on server or workstation in the user's Profiles folder	Always stored on server, on the login server in the mail directory or home directory by default
Function	Replaces USER.DAT entirely	Replaces specified portions of USER.DAT and/or SYSTEM.DAT
Applied	Automatically when user profiles are enabled	Automatically when user profiles are enabled
Created	When users make changes to their application environments and profiles are enabled	When a system administrator runs the Policy Editor and creates a policy file
Editable	By users, any time they change their settings—the settings will be edited to their standing at user logoff	By anyone with access to the Policy Editor

User profiles can control any of the settings stored within HKEY_CURRENT_USER. Setting up user profiles is easy:

1. Activate the Passwords applet in the Control Panel and move to the User Profiles tab.

2. Make sure the option allowing users to customize their preferences is selected.

3. Click OK to exit.

Whenever someone logs onto a computer for the first time, they'll be asked if they want their settings saved for them. If they choose this option, a folder will be created for them in the Windows\Profiles folder, storing their Desktop settings. Any changes made to these settings will be automatically updated and stored when the user logs off.

If you want people to use a certain user profile and not be able to change settings, then you can create a mandatory user profile. Create the settings you want to use, then save USER.DAT as USER.MAN.

WARNING Mandatory user profiles affect every user-specific setting, so use them with discretion.

User profiles may be stored either locally or on the logon server:

- If the logon server is an Windows NT Server computer, you'll need to create a home directory for each user and store their USER.DAT file in it.

- If the logon server is a NetWare computer, then the user profile will be stored in the user's mail directory.

System Policies

Like mandatory user profiles, system policies may be used to mandate user settings. The main difference between the two is that system policies may define only a subset of user settings, whereas user profiles impose a blanket set of user settings by replacing the default USER.DAT.

If you have the Windows 95 CD, you can create system policies with a tool called the Policy Editor (POLEDIT), which you can install using the Add/Remove Programs applet in the Control Panel (see Figure 3.5).

Once you've installed the Policy Editor, you can use it to define the options available for either a specific computer or a specific user. To do so, run the Policy Editor, choose File ➤ New, then select either the computer icon or the user icon depending on which entity you want the policies to apply.

FIGURE 3.5

The Policy Editor gives
you the means to
choose parts of the
environment to control.

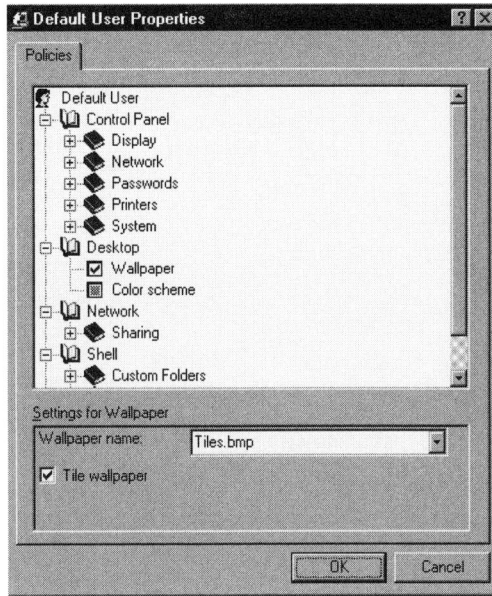

FIGURE 3.5

The Policy Editor gives you the means to choose parts of the environment to control.

The checkboxes in the System Policy Editor determine which options are determined by system policies. Options with a check next to them are enabled in the policy, options with no check are disabled, and options with a gray checkbox (as shown in Figure 3.5) are unaffected by systems policies.

> **NOTE**
>
> By default, Windows 95 automatically downloads system policies from the \NETLOGON folder of the domain controller or the \PUBLIC directory of the preferred server when a user logs on. You can configure it for manual downloading if, for example, you want to store system policy files in an alternate location.

Backing Up and Restoring Data

Backups are an important part of resource management. In this section, we review how to back up and restore data with Windows 95's Backup.

Backing Up Data

To back up your files, run the Backup tool found in the System Tools section of the Accessories folder (see Figure 3.6).

FIGURE 3.6

Windows 95's Backup tool provides a graphical interface for backup operations.

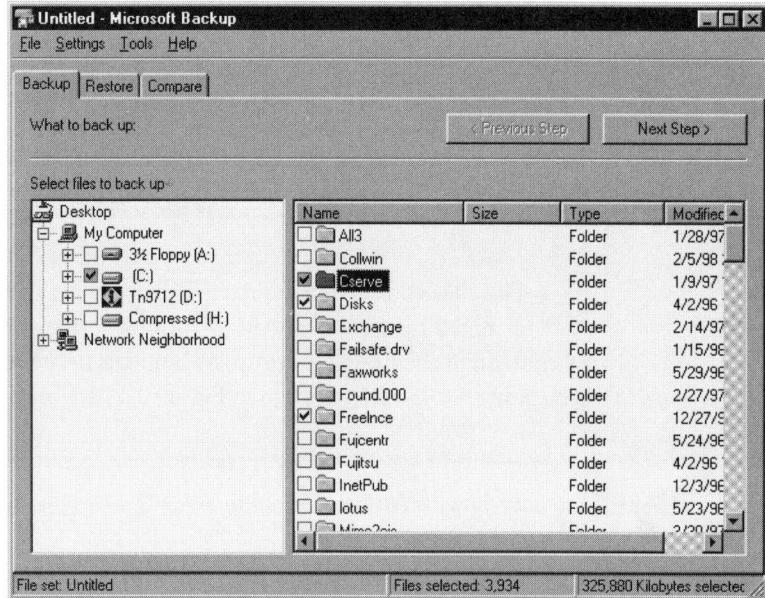

Use the Backup tab (shown in Figure 3.6) to perform backups. Check the boxes of the files or folders you want to back up, and then click the Next Step button to select a destination directory. The destination directory may be a:

- Floppy disk
- Hard disk—local or networked
- Tape drive

TIP

You don't have to back up every file or folder within a main folder. Deselect files that you don't need to back up by clearing their checkboxes.

Name the backup set and assign a password to it if desired, and then click OK.

Windows 95's Backup supports two backup types:

- Full backups

- Incremental backups

Their differences are outlined in Table 3.4.

TABLE 3.4 Full Backups vs. Incremental Backups	**Full Backups**	**Incremental Backups**
	Copy all marked files	Copy all marked files with the archive bit set
	Reset archive bit after copying	Reset archive bit after copying

To perform the same backup operation more than once, create a backup set by selecting both the files to be copied and the destination drive. Save this set using the Save As button so that when you run Backup your files to copy and their destination will already be established.

TIP

Use Windows 95's Backup for backup operations whenever possible, as it supports long file names. DOS-based backup programs do not support long file names, so only the eight-letter aliases will remain. If you *must* use a DOS-based backup program for some reason, you can back up long file names with the LFNBK utility found in the Windows 95 Resource Kit.

Restoring Data

To restore data from backups, run Backup and move to the Restore tab (see Figure 3.7). Select the backup set on the source drive, and then click on Next Step to select the files from the set that you want to restore.

F I G U R E   3.7

Data for restoration is stored in backup sets.

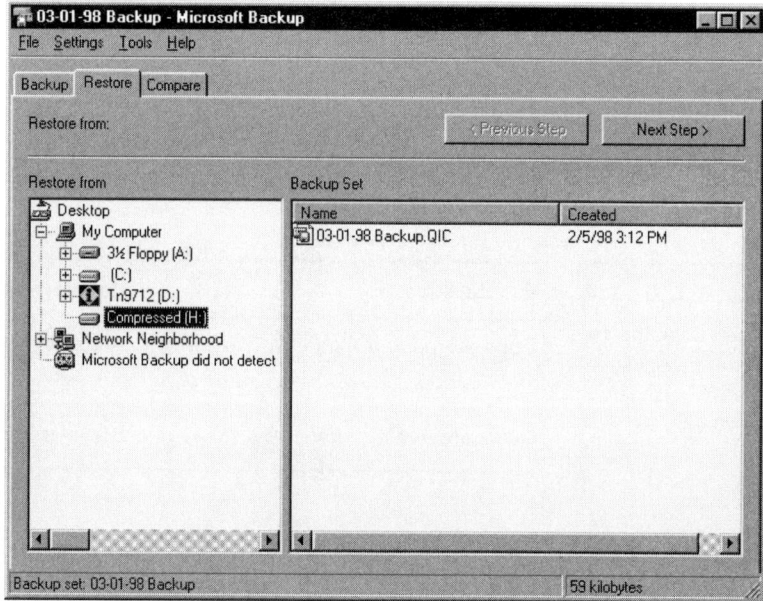

Windows 95 Backup will not restore files that have the same date or an earlier one than an existing file.

If you're not sure whether the contents of the backup set or the files on disk are more recent, you can click on the Compare tab to compare the two. Open a backup set and check the boxes of the files or folders to be compared.

Managing Hard Disks

Windows 95 offers two main hard disk utilities:

- Disk compression
- Disk partitioning

Disk Compression

You can compress drive contents to save space. The degree of compression you achieve depends on the data being compressed; some types of graphics files will compress quite a bit, whereas program files and already compressed files won't compress much at all. Compressed volumes will not be accessible locally from any operating system other than Windows 95.

DriveSpace, the Windows 95 compression utility, is found in the System Tools section of the Accessories folder. Its options are outlined in Table 3.5.

TABLE 3.5 DriveSpace Functions	Function	Description
	Compress	Compresses the selected drive
	Uncompress	Uncompresses the selected drive, expanding all files to their full size
	Adjust Free Space	Shifts free space between a compressed drive and its uncompressed host drive
	Properties	Shows the proportion of free space to unused space on the selected volume
	Format	Formats the selected drive, deleting all data
	Mount	Associates a compressed drive with a compressed volume file (CVF) that contains a map of the compressed volume. A compressed drive must be mounted to be used

TABLE 3.5 *(cont.)*	Function	Description
DriveSpace Functions	Unmount	Disassociates a compressed drive from its CVF
	Create Empty	Creates a new, compressed, logical drive from the space on an uncompressed drive
	Change Ratio	Changes the degree of compression on a drive. The more a volume is compressed, the longer it takes to read from the volume
	Change Letter	Assigns a new drive letter to a volume
	Change Settings	Allows you to determine whether Windows 95 should automatically mount new compressed drives, as is the default

A drive must have a certain amount of free space to be compressed. To save space, you must plan to compress *before* the disk is nearly full.

Disk Partitioning

Disk partitioning is the process of organizing a physical disk into one or more logical drives. To repartition a disk, you'll need a MS-DOS–based utility called FDISK, which is found on the Windows 95 emergency recovery disk or in Windows\Commands. FDISK may be used to accomplish any of the following tasks:

- Creating a new primary MS-DOS partition
- Deleting MS-DOS partitions, logical drives, primary partitions, and extended partitions
- Creating extended partitions and logical drives

These options are explained in Table 3.6.

T A B L E 3.6	Partition Type	Description
Logical Partition Types	Primary partition	The logical drive from which the computer boots
	Extended partition	If the primary partition does not consume all space on the physical disk, the remainder can be defined as an extended partition
	Logical drive	A section of an extended partition to which a drive letter has been assigned. This may be all or part of an extended partition

Although FDISK is an MS-DOS utility, it can run in an MS-DOS window, so long as you're not trying to run it on a physical disk currently in use.

Repartitioning a disk deletes all the data on it. Be sure to back it up before running FDISK.

The options available to you with FDISK are described in Table 3.7.

T A B L E 3.7	Function	Description
FDISK Options	Create partition or logical drive	Create a new logical volume on an existing physical drive
	Set active partition	Specify from which partition the computer should boot
	Delete a partition or logical drive	Destroys a logical volume on a physical disk. Although the disk will not be physically damaged, all data in the deleted partition will be lost because there will be no way to call it back
	Display partition information	Shows how the physical disk is divided into logical partitions, including the size of each

If more than one fixed disk is present, then a fifth option, to change the current fixed drive, will be included in the menu of FDISK options.

Setting Up Application Environments

Under Windows 3.*x*, MS-DOS applications had Program Information Files (PIFs) that configured their operating environments and needed to be edited with a program called PIF Editor. Under Windows 95, all MS-DOS applications have a Properties sheet with which PIFs can be edited. If the standard MS-DOS application settings don't work for a particular application, then you can edit them from the Properties dialog box, which has five sections:

- General
- Program
- Font
- Memory
- Screen
- Miscellaneous

The values for most of these settings are predefined to values that work for most applications, so you may not have to adjust them.

General

The General tab doesn't give you many options other than the ability to set file attributes (see Figure 3.8). It's mostly included to provide file information.

Program

The Program tab is a bit meatier (see Figure 3.9).

In addition to the options on the main part of this tab, you can click on the Advanced button to further define how the program runs (see Figure 3.10).

NOTE   If you run a program in DOS mode, then Windows 95 will shut down but for a small stub, and the application will run as it would under DOS, using all system resources.

FIGURE 3.8

The General tab

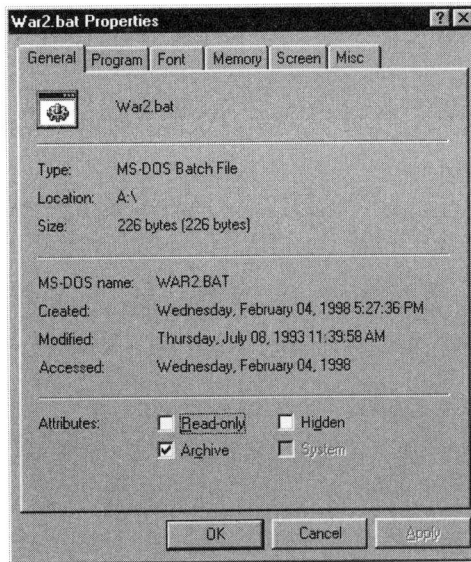

FIGURE 3.9

The Program tab

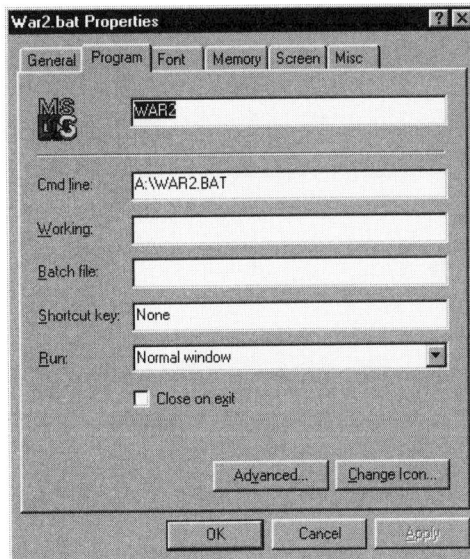

FIGURE 3.10

Advanced Program
Settings for a DOS
application

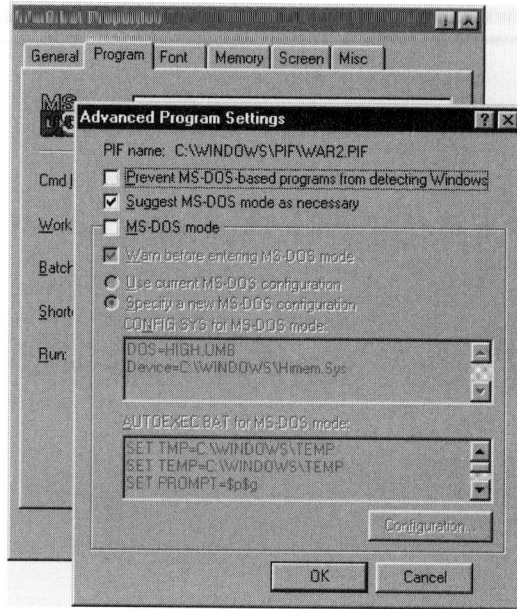

Font

The settings on the Font tab apply to character-based applications (see Figure 3.11).

Memory

The Memory tab lets you manually configure how much of what kind of memory is available to an application (see Figure 3.12).

Table 3.8 briefly describes the types of memory available to DOS applications.

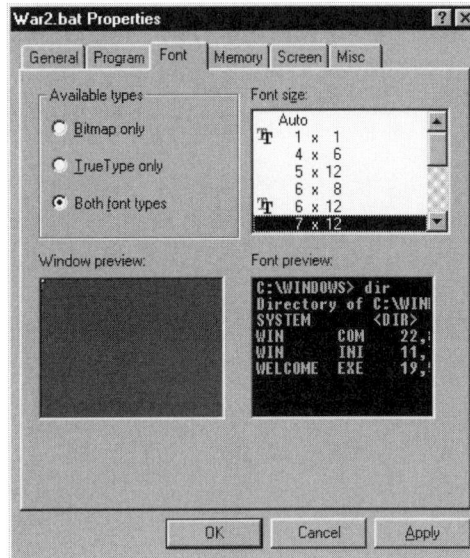

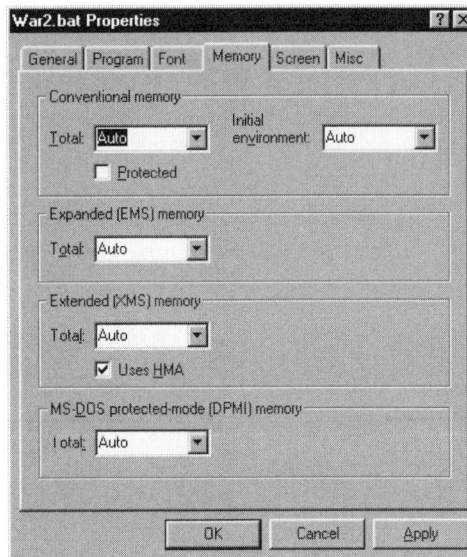

T A B L E 3.8	Type of Memory	Description
DOS Memory Types	Conventional memory	Memory addresses from 0 to 640K, used by all DOS applications
	Extended memory	Memory addresses from 1MB to 4GB, used by some DOS applications
	Expanded memory	Page frames of memory located in the Upper Memory Area (UMA) in the addresses 640KB to 1MB. Data is paged in and out of memory in 16KB pages. Used by some DOS applications, but rarer now that extended memory is available
	DOS Protected Mode Interface (DPMI) memory	Provides a means for DOS applications to run in protected mode when they couldn't ordinarily do so

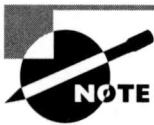

NOTE HIMEM.SYS is required for any programs that use extended memory, as it coordinates the space so that no two programs use the same memory.

Screen

The Screen tab controls the display of the application (see Figure 3.13). Most of the settings are self-explanatory, except for fast ROM and dynamic memory allocation, which are used for display enhancement.

Misc

The Misc tab controls settings that don't really fit in other categories (see Figure 13.14).

FIGURE 3.13

The Screen tab

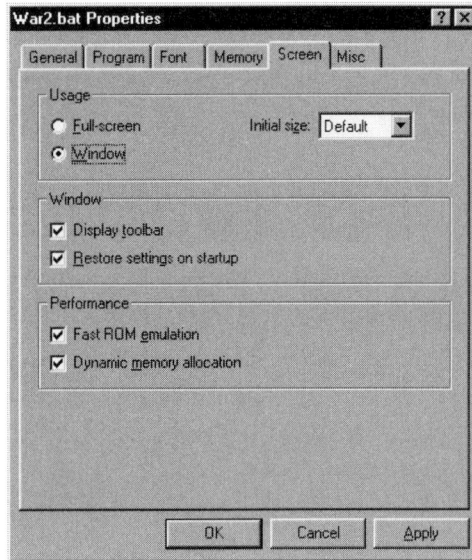

FIGURE 3.14

The Misc tab

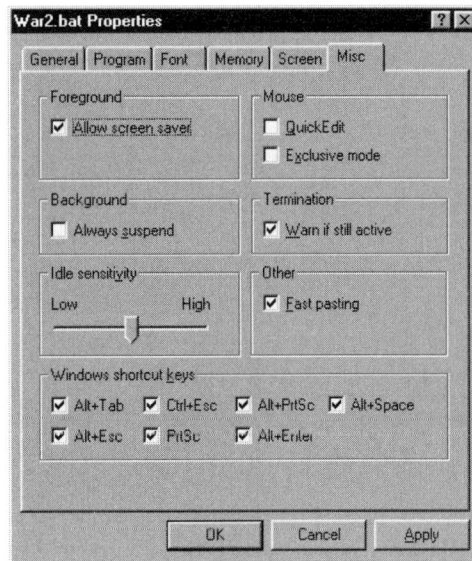

Setting Access Permissions for Shared Folders

1. Mike decides to share his C: drive with other users on the network. What are the three access types Mike can set for the resource?

_____

_____

_____

2. What feature does user-level security rely on?

_____

3. Explain how pass-through authentication verifies user account information.

_____

_____

4. You cannot use Remote Registry services on a peer-to-peer network because they rely on _____ security implementation.

5. True or False: If you have set system policies to require logon validation by a server, Windows 95 becomes a secure system.

6. True or False: You can use a LAN Manager domain controller to provide pass-through security.

7. Which network services support the use of share-level security?

_____

8. What Windows 95 files store Windows logon passwords?

_____

9. Where is the type of security on shared resources specified?

_____

10. What two sorts of security models does the Windows 95 resource sharing support?

_____

_____

11. List the two types of servers that support pass-through authentication.

_____

_____

12. True or False: You can always set passwords for individual shares.

13. Windows 95 relies on _____ to authenticate user requests for resource access.

Creating, Sharing, and Monitoring Network Resources

14. It can take up to _____ minutes for computers to appear and _____ minutes to be removed from the browse list as they are turned on and off.

15. What is wrong with the following UNC name (referencing a Novell file server): \\fs1\sys:\login\login.exe?

_____

16. From the Start menu or the Taskbar, how can you quickly browse a server, even if it does not yet appear in the Network Neighborhood?

_____

17. True or False: To use MS Fax you need to have a fax modem connected to your PC.

18. True or False: Tone or Pulse dialing is a property of each calling location.

19. True or False: UNC naming allows for use of network resources without the need for mapped drives at all.

20. Can you change the applications associated with a particular file extension from within the Network Neighborhood window? If so, how?

_____

21. True or False: You can use MS Fax without installing the Exchange client.

22. What MS Network machines should show up in the default Network Neighborhood screen?

_____

23. True or False: If you have selected to display all file types, the .LNK extension will show up on Shortcuts if you select View ➤ Options and then the View tab (available from any folder window).

24. How can you map a drive without typing in the path?

_____

_____

25. True or False: Drive mappings in Windows 95 are always global across virtual machines.

26. True or False: You can create a file with a name 250 characters long in the C:\DATA\ EXAMPLE directory.

27. How do you share a printer in Windows 95?

_____

_____

28. True or False: The NET VIEW command will browse NetWare servers and workgroups.

29. What is the equivalent UNC name for the \sys\public directory on the computer called MYSERVER?

_____

30. True or False: You can set up shortcuts to servers or network resources.

31. From within the My Computer window, what are the two ways to share the C: drive?

_____

_____

32. You currently have the Network Neighborhood window open and you are informed by a fellow employee that a new server has just been added to the network. Without closing and then re-opening Network Neighborhood, how can you use the mouse to update the window so the new server is shown?

_____

33. True or False: Windows 95 includes automatic optimization of features such as turning off background print rendering in low-memory situations.

34. What is the MSPSRV.EXE file for?

_____

35. How can you change the configuration of Windows 95 so that raw data is sent from the application to the printer driver?

_____

36. List the steps required to install the Microsoft Print Services for NetWare.

_____

_____

_____

37. What would the UNC syntax be to reference the file NWADMIN.EXE in the PUBLIC directory of the SYS volume on the NW410-1 file server?

_____

38. What configuration option must you set to ensure other users on the network can share your fax modem?

_____

39. From the Windows 95 Desktop, the quickest way to map a network drive if you know its UNC path is to right-click on the _____ icon and select the option to Map Network Drive.

40. The "Ghosted Connections" feature of WFWG is similar to what feature of Windows 95?

_____

41. List the following steps in the correct order to create a new directory called C:\EXAMPLE using Explorer.

A. Select File from the menu bar.

B. Enter the name of the desired Folder (directory), EXAMPLE.

C. Select New and then Folder.

D. Highlight the C: drive within the All Folders window.

42. Ruth wants to connect to a folder shared as Working Copy, accessible from server Orion. What would the syntax be to connect to this folder with UNC?

_____

43. Your mail server is stored on a Windows 95 machine. You want to use Windows 95's dial-up server product to provide dial-in connectivity to employees accessing their e-mail from the road or their home office. Will this work? If so, what constraints will exist?

_____

_____

_____

44. To share a fax modem, you must have Microsoft Fax and _____ installed.

45. By default, the security type implemented for shared access to the fax modem is

_____.

Setting Up System Policies and User Profiles

46. Which Registry subtree contains information about users that have logged onto the system?

_____

47. If system policies are to be used in a Windows 95/NetWare environment, the

_____ file must be copied to the

_____ directory on the server.

48. You can specify which template the Policy Editor is using from the

_____ menu.

49. Once installed, where can the System Policy Editor be found within the Start menu?

_____

50. From within the Control Panel, what are the steps required to enable user profiles for a local computer?

_____

_____

_____

51. The System Policy Editor can be used in either the _____

mode or the _____ mode.

52. What feature allows you to change the location in which the Client for Microsoft Networks looks for CONFIG.POL?

_____

53. True or False: User profiles contain all of the Registry HKEY_CURRENT_USER settings.

54. What is the name of the file placed in a secure network location and used to update the Registry on login, and what feature does it implement?

_____

55. Using System Policy Editor, how can you create a new group to which to assign policies?

_____

56. Where are user profiles stored?

_____

57. True or False: USER.DAT supplies the information found in HKEY_USERS.

58. True or False: By default, system policy files are downloaded from \NETLOGON on Windows NT domain controllers and \PUBLIC on NetWare servers.

Backing Up and Restoring Data

59. True or False: Windows 95 Backup can read backup sets from MS-DOS 6.*x* backup utilities.

60. What switch would you use with the LFNBK utility to produce a report of long file names currently in use on your computer?

_____

61. What is a limitation of the differential backup option in Windows 95 Backup?

_____

62. True or False: The QIC 113 tape specification is not supported by Windows 95 because it does not support long file names.

Managing Hard Disks

63. What utility is used to create disk partitions with Windows 95?

_____

64. True or False: You can repartition a hard disk under Windows 95 without destroying the data on that partition.

65. Jim wants to repartition the drives in his computer. In his CONFIG.SYS file, he finds a DEVICE= command referencing a file called SSTOR.SYS. How should this drive be partitioned?

_____

66. The _____ is required to read a compressed volume.

67. True or False: Windows 95 automatically mounts new compressed drives.

68. You've made a new compressed drive from space on an uncompressed one. Now that you've done it, you realize the uncompressed drive doesn't have enough space on it. What option in DriveSpace will permit you to shift free space between drives?

_____

69. True or False: DriveSpace always compresses all files at a ratio of 2:1.

70. True or False: Compressed volumes are only readable from Windows 95, as the compression algorithms are unique to the operating system.

71. You've run out of room on your hard disk, and decide to compress it to give yourself some more room to work. The compression routine fails. Why?

_____

_____

72. Why can't you repartition the boot disk while it's being used?

_____

_____

_____

73. The _____ partition is the one from which the computer will boot.

Setting Up Application Environments

74. If Windows 95 can't find a PIF for an application, it searches the

_____ file for information about the application.

75. _____ memory uses bank switching techniques and

a(n) _____ frame in the Upper Memory Area.

76. True or False: Protected-mode device drivers are loaded in CONFIG.SYS.

77. What is the default value Windows 95 uses for the FILES= setting in CONFIG.SYS?

_____

78. True or False: DPMI memory is used by Windows applications.

79. To alter an application's PIF file settings, you _____ the application.

80. By default, Windows 95 will provide expanded memory to MS-DOS–based applications that require it. What parameter included in CONFIG.SYS would prevent Windows 95 from being able to do this?

_____

81. True or False: Windows 95 creates a DEFAULT.PIF file at installation time.

82. The _____ section of the APPS.INF is used to provide a master listing of settings to be used by MS-DOS applications.

83. What happens to other processes and applications when you elect to run an MS-DOS application in MS-DOS mode?

_____

SAMPLE TEST

3-1   What method of Print Spooling returns control to the application most quickly?

   A. Raw Data Spooling

   B. Enhanced File Spooling

   C. Enhanced Metafile Spooling

   D. Duplex Print Spool (DPS)

3-2   To be able to allow other users on a Novell NetWare network to use a printer on your workstation, what network service must be installed?

   A. File and Print Sharing for Microsoft Networks

   B. File and Print Sharing for NetWare Networks

   C. A and B

   D. None of the above

3-3   Which of the follow commands are correct? Choose all that apply.

   A. `Copy example.doc "Example file"`

   B. `Copy account.txt "March accounts"`

   C. `Copy "January Staffing staff.txt`

   D. `Copy "December bonus" bonus.txt`

3-4   How many UNC connections to network resources does Windows 95 support?

   A. 32

   B. 128

   C. 256

   D. Unlimited

3-5   What do you need to do to allow you to print from MS-DOS applications to a network printer?

    A. Run the Windows 95 CAPTURE utility.

    B. Run the NET CAPTURE PORT command.

    C. Ensure the LPT port has been captured.

    D. All of the above.

3-6   What is the command to browse shared resources from the MS-DOS prompt?

    A. NET BROWSE

    B. NET SHARE

    C. NET VIEW

    D. NET RESOURCE

3-7   How do you set up Windows 95 to require a validated network login (NT or NetWare) before allowing users access to Windows 95?

    A. With system policies

    B. By setting the Primary Network Logon field

    C. A and B

    D. None of the above

3-8   If you have a network with two workgroups, ACCOUNTING and HR, how can you check the browse list for ACCOUNTING?

    A. NET VIEW /WORKGROUP:ACCOUNTING

    B. NET VIEW /MASTER:ACCOUNTING

    C. NET VIEW ACCOUNTING

    D. NET VIEW ACCOUNTING/WORKGROUP

3-9 Which of the following is the recommended minimum configuration to host a workgroup fax machine:

    A. 486-based computer with 4MB of RAM running as a dedicated fax server

    B. 386-based computer with 16MB of RAM running as a dedicated fax server

    C. 486-based computer with 12MB of RAM running as a non-dedicated fax server

    D. 386-based computer with 8MB of RAM running as a dedicated fax server

3-10 What happens if the user profile on the server is newer than the local copy?

    A. The copy on the server is updated.

    B. The local copy is updated.

    C. The user is not allowed to log in.

    D. None of the above.

3-11 Which of the following holds the Compressed Volume File?

    A. An extended partition

    B. A CVF

    C. A logical drive

    D. A host drive

3-12 Which of the following drives can you partition with FDISK without first booting to DOS?

    A. Removable drives only

    B. Removeable drives not presently in use

    C. Any fixed or removeable drive

    D. Any fixed or removeable drive not presently in use

3-13 Which of the following statements are true about compression with Windows 95? Choose all that apply.

   A. By default, Windows 95 associates a compressed drive with a CVF.

   B. An unmounted compressed drive may only be read from the machine on which it was compressed.

   C. You can dynamically shift free space between a compressed volume and an uncompressed one.

   D. You must repartition a disk before creating a new compressed drive.

3-14 Which of the following are not true? Choose all that apply.

   A. User profiles are always loaded locally, whereas system policies may be loaded either locally or from the login server.

   B. System policies may affect both computer settings and user settings, but user profiles are limited to user settings only.

   C. User profiles offer a discretionary amount of control over the system, defining some parameters but permitting users to set others.

   D. System policies apply to both HKEY_CURRENT_USER and HKEY_LOCAL_ MACHINE, but user profiles apply only to HKEY_CURRENT USER.

3-15 When are the settings in USER.DAT applied?

   A. At user login

   B. At system boot

   C. If the user-specific settings in SYSTEM.DAT aren't loaded

   D. None of the above

3-16 You have the default security type set up on your Windows 95 computer and want to restrict access to a particular printer. Which of the following will not work to accomplish this? Choose all that apply.

   A. Share the printer with a dollar sign after its name to hide it in the browse list (PRINTER$).

   B. Set a password on the printer.

   C. Permit only certain individuals or members of certain groups to access the printer.

   D. None of the above.

3-17 Before you can share a resource, you must enable:

   A. Client for Microsoft Networks

   B. File and Print Sharing

   C. User-level sharing

   D. None of the above

3-18 By default, resources shared with the network are:

   A. Unprotected

   B. Protected with user-level permissions

   C. Protected with share-level permissions

   D. Depends on whether it's a client/server or peer/peer network

3-19 Your network is a mixed environment of DOS, Windows 95, and Windows NT machines. Which of the following would be a good share name for a resource to be available to all network clients? Choose all that apply.

    A. NETSHARE

    B. NETWORKSHR

    C. NET SHARE

    D. NET_SHARE

3-20 When setting up a backup operation in Windows 95 Backup, you notice that the checkboxes next to some folders are filled in gray but have a checkbox in them. What does this mean?

    A. That hidden or system files are in the folder and will not be backed up

    B. That the backup set includes files that do not have the archive bit set

    C. That some of the files and folders within the folder are checked to be backed up, but not all

    D. That the backup settings have not changed since the last time a backup was performed

3-21 The bootable partition in a computer is called:

    A. Mounted

    B. Active

    C. Logical

    D. Fixed

UNIT

4

Integration and Interoperability

Test Objectives: Integration and Interoperability

- Configure a Windows 95 computer as a client computer in a Windows NT network.

- Configure a Windows 95 computer as a client computer in a NetWare network.

- Configure a Windows 95 computer to access the Internet.

- Configure a client computer to use Dial-up Networking for remote access in a Microsoft environment and a mixed Microsoft and NetWare environment.

NOTE Exam objectives are subject to change at any time without prior notice and at Microsoft's sole discretion. Please visit Microsoft's Training & Certification Web site (www.microsoft.com/Train_Cert/) for the most current listing of exam objectives.

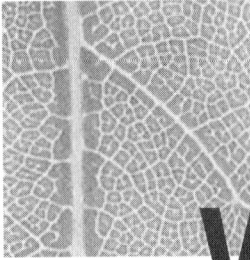

Windows 95 is designed to operate not only on Windows 95 networks but also in a variety of other network environments. Connecting to these environments is mainly a matter of installing the proper client, defining the server to log into, and making sure the client and the server have a common transport protocol.

> **NOTE** Windows 95 supports login scripts for all network types. A login script is a batch file set up to run when a user logs onto the system; it's usually set to configure the user environment. Login scripts must be fairly short to work: Windows NT ones must execute in less than 30 seconds.

Windows 95 and Windows NT

When operating in a mixed NT/Windows 95 network, you can connect to either a domain or a workgroup. Connecting to a domain gives you a unified logon to all domain resources and permits you to automatically download user profiles or system policies at logon, but workgroups can be used when no primary domain controller exists.

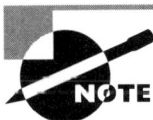

> **NOTE** To access user profiles or system policies stored on a Windows NT primary domain controller, you must set up Windows 95 to validate your logon through its domain.

Installing the Client for Microsoft Networks

The first step to using Windows 95 and Windows NT together is to install the Client for Microsoft Networks, if not already installed. In the Network applet in the Control Panel, turn to the Configuration tab and click the Add button. You'll be presented with list of component types from which to choose. Choose Client, and then choose Microsoft for the manufacturer and the Client for Microsoft Networks as the product (see Figure 4.1).

FIGURE 4.1

Installing the Client for Microsoft Networks

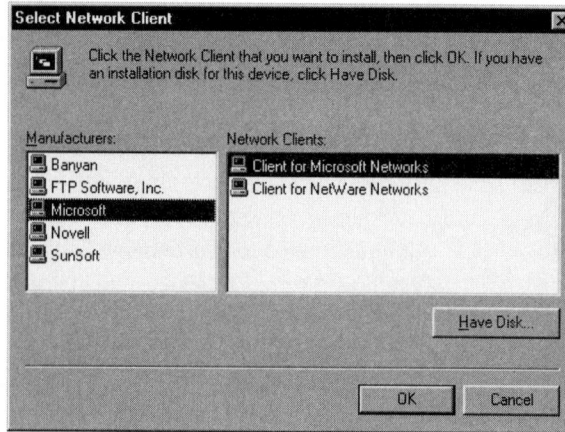

Once the client is installed, you need to specify the domain in which the user has an account so he or she can log in. You'll do this with the Properties button available when the Client for Microsoft Networks is selected. In the Properties dialog box, supply either the name of the primary domain controller holding the user database for the domain you're logging into, or the Windows NT workstation or server to which you'll be logging in directly and on which you have an account (see Figure 4.2).

With the Client for Microsoft Networks installed, all that's required is that you install a common protocol for use on the network. You can use NetBEUI, IPX/SPX-compatible protocol, or TCP/IP to connect to a Windows NT machine.

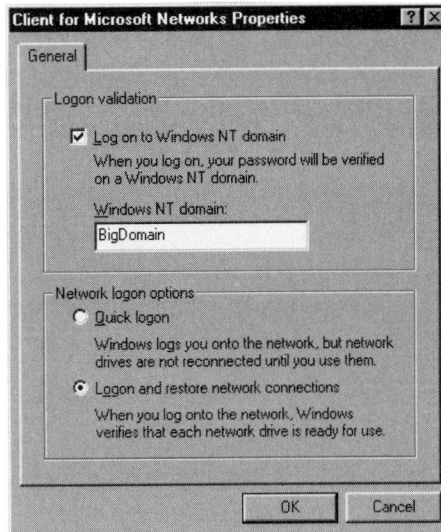

Windows 95 and NetWare

Configuring Windows 95 to work with NetWare is a bit more complicated than getting it to work with Windows NT. You must choose a client type, set up support for long file names, and configure pass-through authentication.

> When set up for NetWare networking, the value of LastDrive set in the Registry is 32, instead of the 26 used with Microsoft networking. The six extra drives are only available to NetWare applications, however, not users.

Choosing a Client Type

When running Windows 95 in combination with NetWare, you have a choice of three clients:

- The Client for NetWare Networks
- NETX
- VLM

NOTE

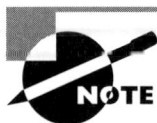

The Client for NetWare Networks runs with the IPX/SPX-compatible transport protocol and with NDIS 3.1 protected-mode drivers, whereas NETX and VLM support NetWare IP and use ODI real-mode drivers.

These clients are compared in Table 4.1.

T A B L E 4.1: Clients for NetWare

Client Name	Runs In...	Application	Advantage
Client for NetWare Networks	Protected mode	May be used to attach to all NetWare networks (2.15 and later) using bindery directory services or bindery emulation	Faster than real-mode clients, uses no conventional memory, supports long file names and client-side caching, automatically recreates connections, supports user profiles
NETX	Real mode	May be used to attach to all NetWare 3.x networks	Supports all NetWare functions not supported by the Microsoft client, including NetWare IP
VLM	Real mode	May be used to attach to all NetWare 4.x networks	Supports all NetWare functions (including NDS and NetWare IP) not supported by the Microsoft client

You can install the Client for NetWare Networks either during installation or afterward. When you install the Client for NetWare Networks, Windows 95 updates the Registry with any settings stored in NET.CFG, using this information to configure other network components.

To set up the Client for NetWare Networks, open the Network applet in the Control Panel and turn to the Configuration tab. If NETX or VLM is installed, select them in the list and click Remove to uninstall them, to make sure that Windows 95 upgrades the entire NetWare stack. Click the Add button, then choose to install a client. Choose Microsoft from the Manufacturers list and Client for NetWare Networks from the list of clients.

NetWare Protocol Configuration

To access NetWare networks, you must have the IPX/SPX-compatible protocol installed, and you may have to do some configuring of the following protocol properties, accessible by selecting the protocol in the list of installed components and clicking the Properties button.

Frame Type

When using IPX/SPX, you must specify how the data is packaged on the datalink level—that is, what its frame type is. Not all NetWare network servers use the same frame type. NetWare 3.12 and later use the 802.2 type, but previous versions use 802.3. Ordinarily, this isn't something you have to be concerned with. When an Windows 95 IPX/SPX node joins the network, it sends out a Routing Information Protocol (RIP) packet to find out what kind of packets are needed on the network, and based on the responses it gets back from all the NetWare servers, it will use the frame type in most common use.

Note that Windows 95 will use the frame type in most common use, not all possible frame types. Autodetection is done once per network session, not every time a packet is sent or received.

If all the servers use the same frame type, this is fine. If you can't connect to a particular server, however, and you know that it uses a different frame type from the others, you may need to manually specify a frame type.

NetBIOS over IPX/SPX

If you're running applications that require NetBIOS, you can still run them on a NetWare network by enabling NetBIOS over IPX/SPX.

Network Address

Each node on an IPX/SPX network has a two-part address that consists of a computer number and a network number. You can either specify a network number on the Advanced tab, or leave it at its default value of 0 to let SAP and RIP automatically determine the network number.

Configuring Pass-Through Authentication

When using Windows 95 with NetWare networks and user-level security, you'll need to specify a preferred server (for logging onto the network) and a security provider for pass-through authentication. The two servers do not need to be the same; one can be the login computer and one can hold the security database. The latter must have an account called WINDOWS_PASSTHRU, a special account used for validation. The process of pass-through authentication goes like this:

1. The client asked to be granted access to the Windows 95 resource, offering as its credentials its username and password.

2. The Windows 95 user-level security server forwards the request and credentials to the NetWare security provider.

3. The NetWare security provider compares the credentials against its accounts database, the bindery.

4. If it passes muster, the NetWare security provider informs the Windows 95 server that the client's credentials are valid.

5. The Windows 95 server grants the client access to the resource based on the access supplied to that user.

> **NOTE**   When you make the Client for NetWare Networks the primary logon, then you'll be prompted for the name of the preferred server.

Making Windows 95 Resources Available to the NetWare Network

Making Windows 95 resources available to NetWare computers takes a little preparation. You must:

- Install File and Print Services for NetWare to make the resources available.

- Specify a NetWare server for pass-through authentication.

- Enable SAP advertising, used by NetWare networks to browse available resources.

The first time you log onto a NetWare network from a Windows 95 machine, you'll be prompted for your NetWare password. If this password and your Windows 95 password are identical, then you'll only have one login step in future.

Enabling Support for Long File Names

NetWare does not support long file names on its own. You must make a Net-Ware volume emulate an HPFS volume to store files with long names (such as user profiles) on it:

1. On the NetWare server, type the following at the command prompt:

   load os2

   add name space os2 to volume sys

2. Add the line **load os2** to STARTUP.NCF for the NetWare server.

3. Shut down the file server, then copy OS2.NAM from the NetWare disks or CD to the same directory on the NetWare file server in which SERVER.EXE is located.

4. Restart the file server.

By default, Windows 95 supports long file names on any volume capable of using them.

Windows 95 and the Internet

Windows 95 offers three ways to get to the Internet:

- You can join the Microsoft Network (MSN), available from the Desktop.

- You can install TCP/IP to configure your computer for dial-up access to an Internet provider.

- You can install TCP/IP and a network card to connect to a computer that has an Internet connection.

> **NOTE** You need to install TCP/IP for Internet access because that's the protocol used on the Internet network. It's a network like any other, in that you must use the protocol in use by everyone else to send and receive data.

Connecting to the Internet

To connect to the Internet without using MSN, follow these steps:

1. Get an account with an Internet service provider (ISP). Preferably, this account should use the Point to Point Protocol (PPP), which is faster and simpler to use, but Windows 95 also supports the Serial Line Internet Protocol (SLIP).

2. Install a modem.

3. Install TCP/IP.

4. Install Dial-up Networking, either specifying the IP address of the Domain Name Service server or plugging in the IP address that was given to you.

Installing TCP/IP

Install TCP/IP from the Network applet in the Control Panel (see Figure 4.3).
Click on the Add button shown here, then, in the dialog box that appears, choose to add a protocol (see Figure 4.4).
As you select each manufactuers' name, the protocols available for each appear in the opposing column.

> **NOTE** Windows 95 supports several manufacturers' transport protocols; TCP/IP is a Microsoft protocol.

Creating a Dial-up Networking Connection

When the modem and the transport protocol are installed, the final step is to create the connection. To get started, open the Dial-up Networking (DUN) folder available from My Computer, and right-click on the Make New Connection icon to create a new set of dial-up settings. You'll open a wizard like the one shown in Figure 4.5.

FIGURE 4.3

Installing TCP/IP

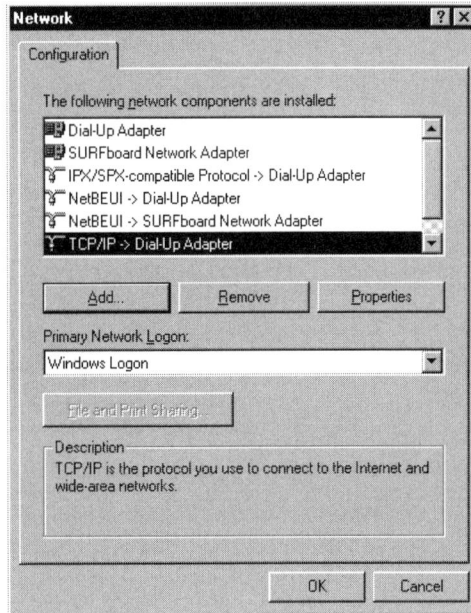

FIGURE 4.4

Choosing a transport
protocol to install

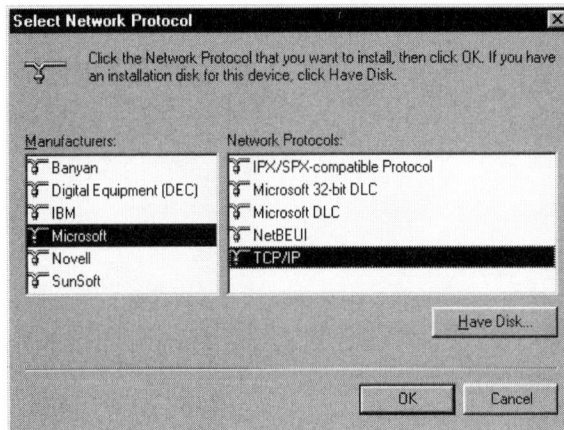

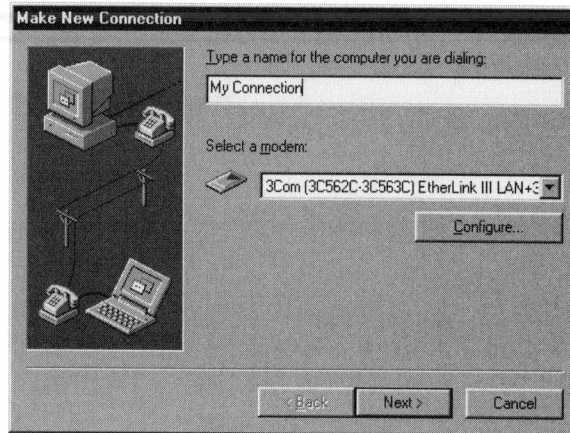

From here, you'll simply pick a modem to connect with, plug in the telephone number to dial, and name the connection.

The Make New Connection Wizard only creates a new connection, however—it doesn't configure it. To do so, right-click on the new connection's
icon in the DUN folder and choose Properties from the pop-up menu to open
the dialog box (see Figure 4.6).

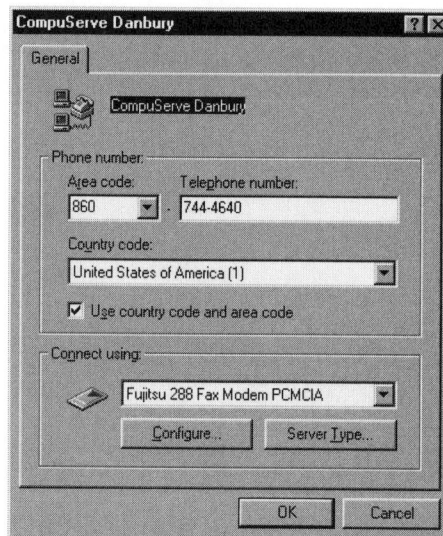

To enter the DNS server's IP address (or your own computer's IP address, if you have one), click on the Server Type button (shown in Figure 4.6) and then choose to configure TCP/IP properties (see Figure 4.7).

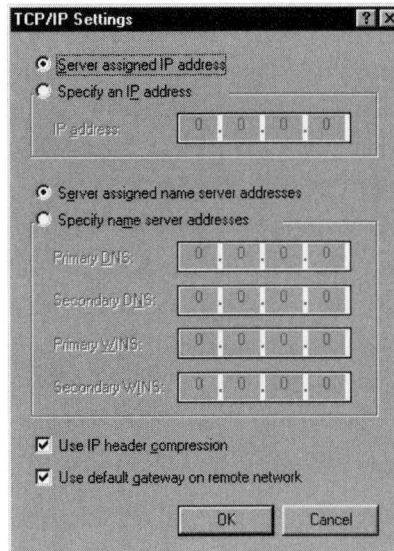

Fill out these blanks as follows:

- If your computer has a static IP address, then fill in the top section.

- If your computer is assigned an address from a Domain Name Service (DNS) server, then fill in the IP addresses of the primary and backup DNS servers.

- If your network is using WINS (unlikely for this scenario) for name resolution, then fill in the IP address in the appropriate section.

NOTE

Most Internet service providers automatically assign you an IP address, and some also automatically assign the DNS server addresses.

Windows 95 and Dial-Up Networking for Remote Access

Windows 95 machines may act as dial-up clients for a variety of network types:

- Windows NT
- LAN Manager
- NetWare
- Windows 95

To use a dial-up connection from a Windows 95 client, the machine must have dial-up networking installed, be using the appropriate client type, and have a transport protocol in common with the server to which it's connecting.

You can install limited RAS server software for Windows 95 from the Microsoft Plus CD. Both server and client must have the Client for Microsoft Networks installed, both must be using Dial-up Networking, and both must be running a common transport protocol—either NetBEUI or IPX/SPX. File and Printer Sharing for Microsoft Networks must also be installed on the server, and Dial-up Networking on the server must have Allow Caller Access enabled.

Only the following machines may connect to a Windows 95 dial-up server:

- Windows NT
- Windows 95
- Windows for Workgroups 3.11

Remote Access Types

You can make two types of remote access connections:

- Explicit—manually started from DUN.
- Implicit—started when you do something that requires Windows 95 to make the connection.

- Application—some applications (such as e-mail programs and Web browsers) can sense when a network connection is needed, and can be configured to create a connection if one is not already active.

To create an explicit connection, create a new connection in DUN, specifying the name of the connection and the telephone number to dial. To use this connection, you'd double-click on it from the DUN folder.

An implicit connection is attempted when you or an application attempt to access a resource via a UNC path, such as when attempting to access a printer or network server. If Windows 95 can't make the connection on the network, then it will prompt you to attempt to make the connection via DUN.

> Implicit connections are not made when a resource is mapped to a specific drive letter. If such a resource is unavailable, then Windows 95 will report that it can't access the resource.

In either case, when making the connection you'll be prompted for your username and password according to the account you have on the dial-up server.

Supported Protocol Types

Making a local area network connection requires a network protocol such as NetBEUI or TCP/IP. To make the connection to a dial-up server, you need two types of protocols: a line protocol and a data protocol. The data protocol packages the data from an application and readies it for transmission; the line protocol transports the packets on the dial-up network.

Data protocols are largely the same as the transport protocols used in Windows 95 networking; the dial-up client supports NetBEUI, IPX/SPX-compatible protocol, and TCP/IP. Supported line protocols include:

- PPP

- SLIP

- A RAS client (listed as Windows for Workgroups and Windows NT 3.1)

- NetWare's NetWare Connect (listed as NRN)

You can use these protocols as outlined in Table 4.2.

T A B L E 4.2	To Remotely Access These Servers...	Use This Data Protocol	And This Line Protocol
Choosing a Line and Data Control	An older Internet connection	TCP/IP	SLIP
	NetWare Servers	IPX/SPX-compatible protocol	NRN
	The Internet	TCP/IP	PPP
	Windows 95 Dial-Up Servers	NetBEUI or IPX/SPX-compatible protocol	PPP
	Windows for Workgroups	NetBEUI	RAS
	Windows NT 3.1	NetBEUI	RAS
	Windows NT 3.5 and later	TCP/IP, NetBEUI, or IPX/SPX-compatible	PPP

If the server you're dialing into supports either PPP or RAS, then you don't have to worry about choosing a line protocol, as Windows 95 will first attempt to make the connection with PPP and then with RAS if PPP doesn't work. Only SLIP and NRN connections must be explicitly selected; Windows 95 will not automatically try these line protocols.

Once you're in, you have access to the network of the type determined by the dial-up server. For example, if you dial into a Windows NT dial-up server and are permitted access to the network, you'll have access to the network just as you would if accessing it locally.

Of course, to access a server type, you must have the appropriate client installed just as you would to access it on a local network.

Connecting to NetWare Resources

Windows 95's DUN client lets you remotely access NetWare resources in any of four ways:

- Connecting to a NetWare Connect server

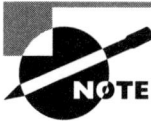

> **NOTE**
>
> If you connect to a NetWare Connect server with DUN, you only get the remote access capabilities of NetWare Connect, not modem pooling or remote control.

- Connecting to a Windows 95 dial-up server running IPX/SPX and with access to NetWare servers
- Connecting to a Windows NT network with the Gateway Services for NetWare installed
- Connecting to a dial-up router with access to a NetWare network

Windows 95 and Windows NT

1. The Microsoft network is only used to download system policies and profiles if the Client for Microsoft Networks is set as the _____.

2. What is the name of the redirector file used by the Client for Microsoft Networks?

_____

3. True or False: Windows 95 offers a single unified login that can be used for all 32-bit network clients.

4. What two server services does Windows 95 ship with?

_____

_____

5. What sort of network login scripts does Windows 95 support?

_____

6. True or False: To be validated by an NT Domain, the Windows 95 machine needs to have its workgroup name set to that of the domain name.

Windows 95 and NetWare

7. What essential information is required to support Primary Logon to NetWare?

_____

8. True or False: The Windows 95 Setup program only installs the Client for NetWare Networks if it detects NetWare components currently present.

9. Windows 95 will not install the Client for NetWare Networks if it detects the NetWare _____ currently installed using NDS support.

10. True or False: You can use Windows 95's File and Print Services for NetWare without a NetWare file server.

11. True or False: Windows 95 supports running several File and Print Service providers at once.

12. What three key things must be done to allow Novell NetWare clients to see shared resources on Windows 95 machines?

_____

_____

_____

13. True or False: Windows 95 will by default attempt to use the current username and password to log into a NetWare server when one is accessed.

14. Describe a key difference related to the mapping of login directories in the behavior of MS Client for NetWare login and Novell's LOGIN.EXE.

_____

15.   True or False: Microsoft's protected-mode NetWare login script processor will load TSRs from the login script.

16.   When using the Client for NetWare Networks, what settings are required in the AUTOEXEC.BAT file?

_____

17.   True or False: You should use Novell's LOGIN.EXE program with MS Client for NetWare.

18.   True or False: The Client for NetWare Networks can be installed in conjunction with the DOS Requester (VLMs).

19.   How much conventional memory does the Client for Microsoft Networks require?

_____

20.   What client must you use to support NCP Packet Signatures from a NetWare server?

_____

21.   How many drive mappings does Microsoft's Client for NetWare support?

_____

22.   True or False: Microsoft's NetWare client supports the use of IP for NetWare connectivity and NCP packet signature.

23. What versions of NetWare are supported with the Client for NetWare Networks?

_____

24. True or False: The Client for NetWare Networks that ships with Windows 95 supports NDS.

25. For the best print server performance, the _____
option for the Microsoft Print Services for NetWare should be set to
_____ seconds.

26. When a Windows 95 workstation is using the Client for NetWare Networks, the user is asked to enter the username and password twice, once for Windows and once for the NetWare server. Why does he have to enter his ID and password twice?

_____

27. If Sally's NetWare server is not configured to support long file names, how will this impact her user profiles?

_____

28. List the NetWare clients that Windows 95 ships with and the mode in which each one runs.

_____

_____

_____

29.   You're connecting to a NetWare 4.*x* network and want to use a real-mode client. What client will you use, and what frame type?

_____

_____

30.   The _____ Windows 95 client supports NDS.

31.   True or False: You cannot use NetWare IP with Windows 95, but must use IPX/SPX-compatible protocol to connect to the network.

32.   True or False: You can support both user profiles and NetWare IP at the same time.

33.   The _____ protocol is used to determine the frame type to use when a Windows 95 computer joins a NetWare network.

Windows 95 and the Internet

34.   Are the options you choose for the dialing properties of the Windows 95 Dial-up Networking stored in the Registry? If not, where are they stored?

_____

35.   When configuring your dial-up connection, in the Server Types window, you selected the Log on to Network option. By default, what ID will Windows use to try and log you in?

_____

36. True or False: Windows 95 allows for manually entering commands before or after dialing.

37. For what reason would you select the Bring up Terminal Window before Dialing option within a modem's Properties dialog box?

_____

38. When it comes to modem configuration, what characters specify a two-second pause and a user prompt?

_____

39. When configuring your Internet connection, if the service provider does not have a DHCP or BOOTP server, you will need to know the IP subnet mask, the _____ IP address and your own IP address.

40. Where in the TCP/IP Properties dialog box do you specify the DNS host name?

_____

41. Susan purchased Windows 95 on floppy diskette and installed it on her computer with 16MB of RAM and a 200MB hard drive. This computer is equipped with a 14.4Kbps modem. What must she do to configure Dial-up Networking to establish a SLIP connection using her copy of Windows 95?

_____

42. The IP address for ftp.microsoft.com is 198.105.232.1. To test your connection with the Internet and to ensure that your TCP/IP stack is functioning properly, you can use the command ping 198.105.232.1. What command can you use to test your connection to the DNS server?

_____

43. Internet Control Message Protocol (ICMP) echo packets are sent by which utility to verify a connection?

_____

Windows 95 and Dial-up Networking for Remote Access

44. True or False: To access a server's UNC name via DUN, you must first open the DUN folder and activate a connection to that server.

45. True or False: To connect to a NetWare server via DUN, you must use NRN, the Windows 95 version of NetWare Connect.

46. PPP is one example of a _____ protocol.

47. List the data protocols supported for DUN.

_____

_____

_____

48. Explain the difference between a line protocol and a data protocol.

_____

_____

49. The dial-up Windows NT Server you connect to has finally been upgraded from Windows NT 3.1 to Windows NT 4.0. The line protocol is still set on the default setting and has never been adjusted. Do you need to specify a new line protocol? Why or why not?

_____

_____

_____

_____

50. A user wants to access a Windows 95 machine via a dial-up connection. What Microsoft product allows this?

_____

51. From within the Phone Dialer utility, how can you access the Dialing Properties?

_____

52. After establishing a dial-up connection, from the Desktop, how can you determine which protocols are currently active?

_____

53. List the connection protocols that Dial-up Networking supports.

_____

_____

_____

_____

54. List the transport protocols that can be used with PPP.

_____

_____

_____

55. What steps must you take to enable Dial-up Networking?

_____

56. List the methods of name resolution that Windows 95 TCP/IP internetworks support.

_____

_____

_____

_____

57. True or False: Windows 95 ships with a dial-up server.

58. List the dial-up servers Windows 95 supports.

_____

_____

_____

_____

59. True or False: Windows 95 supports software compression on Dial-up Networking.

60. With what Server Services does Windows 95 ship?

_____

61. True or False: Windows 95 can act as an IP router.

62. True or False: After entering the IP address for a gateway, you must press Enter to have the address added to the listing of Installed Gateways.

SAMPLE TEST

4-1 Which protocol must be bound to your dial-up adapter to be able to access the Internet?

    A. NetBEUI

    B. IPX/SPX

    C. TCP/IP

    D. A and C

4-2 Windows 95 File and Print Services for NetWare supports two mechanisms for advertising shared resources. What are they? Choose all that apply.

    A. Workgroup Advertising

    B. File Advertising

    C. FPS Advertising

    D. SAP Advertising

4-3 How many NetWare servers can Windows 95 obtain a list of users from for pass-through authentication?

    A. 1

    B. 2

    C. 5

    D. None

4-4 What do you have to do if using login scripts for Microsoft Networks on networks that have both primary and backup domain controllers?

    A. A copy of the login script should be copied to the \Windows\System directory.

    B. A copy of the login script should be copied to every domain controller.

C. A copy of the login script should be copied to the \Windows directory.

D. None of the above.

4-5 What is the IP configuration information utility that ships with Windows 95 called?

A. IPCONFIG

B. WINIP

C. WINIPCFG

D. CNFGIP

4-6 How many WINS servers can be specified?

A. One—A primary

B. Two—A primary and a secondary

C. Three—A primary, secondary, and tertiary

D. None of the above

4-7 Windows 95 can automatically download system policies from a NetWare server. Which client must be used for this to occur? Choose all that apply.

A. VLMs

B. DOS Requester

C. Microsoft Client for NetWare Networks

D. NETX

E. Microsoft Client for Microsoft Networks

SAMPLE TEST

4-8 When must you specify the frame type used on NetWare networks? Choose all that apply.

    A. Always.

    B. You're connecting to NetWare 2.15 servers.

    C. SAP advertising fails.

    D. None of the above.

4-9 Choose all that apply. To support NDS access, you must install:

    A. VLM.

    B. NETX.

    C. Client for NetWare Networks.

    D. Windows 95 does not support NDS access.

4-10 What is the default network number specified on Windows 95 for NetWare networks?

    A. 0.

    B. 1.

    C. 2.

    D. There is no default.

4-11 What is the purpose of running NetBIOS over IPX/SPX?

    A. It speeds up data transmission time as NetBIOS is a faster protocol.

    B. It permits routing of NetBIOS traffic for other clients.

    C. It permits network applications that require access to the NetBIOS commands to run on a NetWare network.

    D. It takes over in case of failure of the main protocol, so transmissions can still get through.

4-12   Which of the following does Windows 95 support for use as a data protocol? Choose all that apply.

> **A.** PPP
>
> **B.** TCP/IP
>
> **C.** DLC
>
> **D.** NetBEUI

4-13   Which of the following line protocols can you use to connect to the Internet?

> **A.** PPP
>
> **B.** TCP/IP
>
> **C.** SLIP
>
> **D.** NetBEUI

4-14   When is an implicit DUN connection made? Choose all that apply.

> **A.** When you access a UNC path not available on the local network
>
> **B.** When you access a drive letter mapped to a resource not available on the local network
>
> **C.** When you double-click a connection in the Dial-up Networking folder
>
> **D.** When you start an application that requires an Internet connection

4-15   When accessing a NetWare server across a dial-up connection, which Windows 95 line protocol should you use?

   A. TCP/IP

   B. PPP

   C. NRN

   D. NetWare Connect

4-16   Which of the following should you use to connect to a Windows NT 3.1 server?

   A. PPP.

   B. SLIP.

   C. RAS.

   D. Windows NT 3.1 does not support dial-up services.

4-17   Which of the following actions is unnecessary to connect to a Windows NT 4.0 computer via a dial-up connection? Choose all that apply.

   A. Installing the Client for Microsoft Networks

   B. Specifying PPP as the line protocol

   C. Choosing a data protocol

   D. None of the above

UNIT

5

Monitoring and Optimization

Test Objectives: Monitoring and Optimization

- Monitor system performance. Tools include:
  - NetWatcher
  - System Monitor

- Tune and optimize the system in a Microsoft environment and a mixed Microsoft and NetWare environment. Tools include:
  - Disk Defragmenter
  - ScanDisk
  - DriveSpace

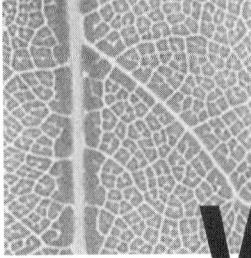

Windows 95 comes with several tools you can use to get the most out of your system resources. This unit reviews how those tools are used.

Monitoring System Performance

Two of the monitoring tools that Windows 95 comes with are Net-Watcher and the System Monitor:

NetWatcher allows local and remote management of users' connections to Windows 95 peer services such as file and printer sharing. It shows who's connected and permits you to break those connections. It also maintains a log of related events, such as logon and logoff, system shutdown, and failed attempts to connect to resources.

System Monitor diagnoses performance problems on a local or remote computer. It covers the gamut of system operations, including hardware, software services, and applications.

NetWatcher

NetWatcher is Windows 95's peer network resource manager. With this tool, you can:

- Add a shared resource or quit sharing a resource.

- Show all shared resources on a computer, view the users connected to those resources, and determine which files are open.

- Close files that users have opened.

- Disconnect users from resources.

Whether you're using share-level security or user-level security, Net-Watcher still works. There are a couple of caveats to this:

- If you're using share-level security you can only remotely administer other share-level computers, whereas if you're using user-level security you can connect to any Windows 95 machine with the Remote Registry service running, even if the two computers use different computers for pass-through authentication.

- Computers running File and Print Sharing for NetWare Networks can only connect to other computers running File and Print Sharing for NetWare Networks.

- The computers to be monitored must be running the File and Print Sharing services.

- On NetWare networks, NetWatcher does not allow you to close files on remote computers, although you can disconnect users.

NOTE The Remote Registry service must be running on all computers to be monitored. To keep users from tampering with other users' network access, you can permit only certain users or groups to use the tools associated with the Remote Registry service. By default, this right is limited to those with administrative privileges.

To administer a remote computer with NetWatcher, run NETWATCH.EXE and choose to connect to a server. Provide the password required (if it's a share-level security computer, the password will be the Remote Administration password specified in the Control Panel; if it's a user-level security computer, the password will be that of the Administrator account specified in the Passwords applet of the Control Panel). You should now be connected (see Figure 5.1).

FIGURE 5.1

Use NetWatcher to
remotely administer
peer resources.

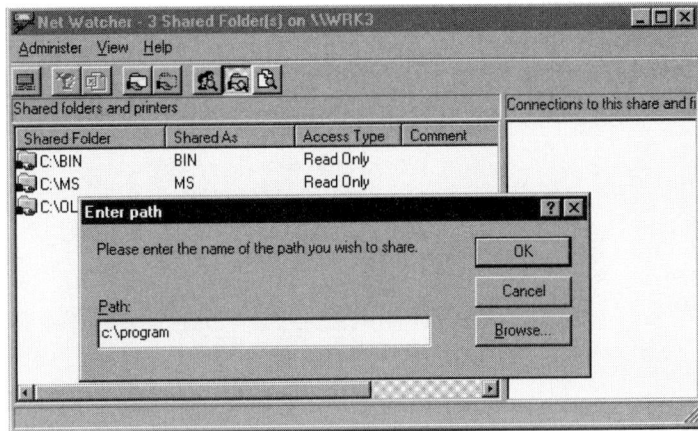

FIGURE 5.1

Use NetWatcher to remotely administer peer resources.

System Monitor

Windows 95's System Monitor keep tabs on a number of different aspects of the system and notices changes that could signal problems.

To install System Monitor, open the Add/Remove Programs applet in the Control Panel and move to the Windows Setup tab. Check Accessories, and click the Details button to view the list of installed components. Make sure System Monitor is checked, and click OK.

> The System Monitor utility is located in the System Tools section of the Accessories folder. Alternatively, you can run it by typing **sysmon** in the Run utility.

The System Monitor affords a number of performance counters, arranged by category (see Figure 5.2). You can monitor as many of these counters as you like, remembering that running the System Monitor will incur a performance hit as the utility uses system resources.

Table 5.1 lists the counter categories and explains what's covered under each.

FIGURE 5.2

Choose a category and then choose counters within that category.

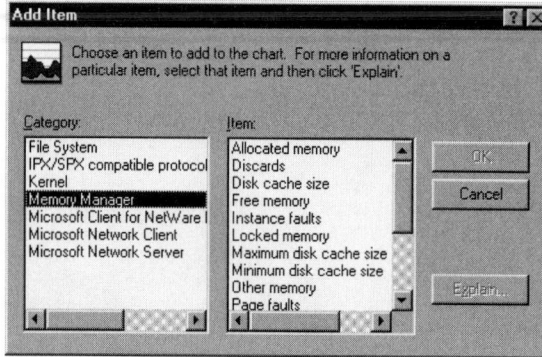

TABLE 5.1

Counter Categories

Category	Description
File System	Measures, reads, and writes to the system per second (both in terms of the number of bytes read or written, and the number of reads and writes) and the amount of data waiting to be written to disk
IPX/SPX-Compatible Protocol	Monitors IPX/SPX packets sent, received, and lost. Can also monitor the number of free sockets, known routes, and service advertisements
Kernel	Monitors Kernel activity, including how often the processor is busy, how many threads are currently running (a *thread* is the smallest unit of software), and how many virtual machines are present in the system
Memory Manager	Measures everything to do with memory management: swap file size, minimum and maximum disk cache size, page faults, pages discarded, allocated memory, and free physical memory
Microsoft Client for NetWare Networks	All network data for a NetWare network, including bytes read and written per second, the amount of cached data, pending requests, and dropped packets

T A B L E 5.1 *(cont.)* Counter Categories	Category	Description
	Microsoft Network Client	All network data for a Microsoft network, including the bytes read and written per second, the number of networks running, the number of open files, resources, and active sessions, and the number of SMB transactions per second
	Microsoft Network Server	All network data for file and print sharing, including the bytes read from and written to disk, the number of buffers, threads, and memory used by the server and the number of server network buffers
	Microsoft Network Monitor	Records network data for the network type (Token Ring or Ethernet), including the number of broadcast frames transmitted per second and the total numbers of bytes, frames, and multicast frames transmitted over the network adapter per second

The Microsoft Network Client and Microsoft Network Server categories relate respectively to the Client for Microsoft Networks and to File and Print Sharing.

As you add counters, the display of the System Monitor will change to display them all, as shown in Figure 5.3.

The information you garner from these counters can help you determine whether some kind of hardware adjustment is necessary. For example, if your system experiences a high number of page faults (pages being recalled from the virtual memory area on disk), then more physical memory might help speed up performance. Table 5.2 lists some potential problems and the System Monitor counter that you might use to identify them.

To run the System Monitor on a remote machine, that machine must have the Remote Registry Service installed.

FIGURE 5.3

Active counters in the
System Monitor

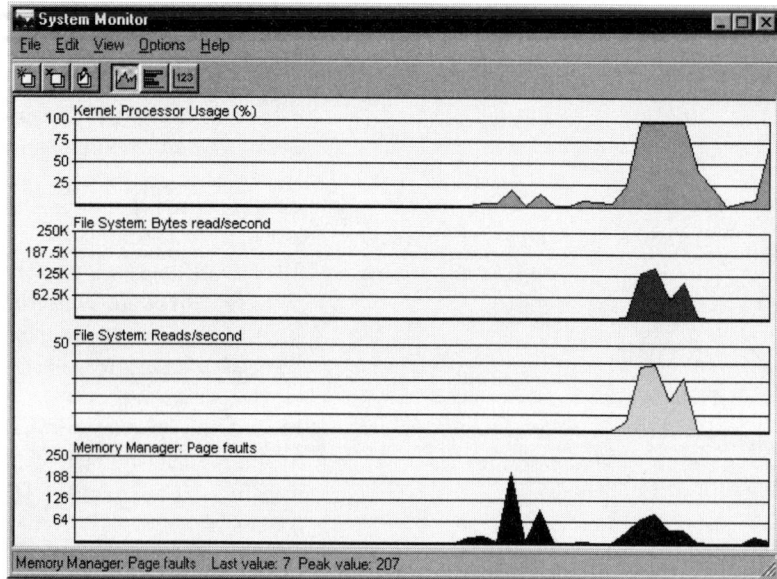

System Monitor screenshot showing:
- Kernel: Processor Usage (%)
- File System: Bytes read/second
- File System: Reads/second
- Memory Manager: Page faults — Last value: 7 Peak value: 207

T A B L E 5.2 Troubleshooting with the System Monitor	**This Counter...**	**May Highlight This Problem...**
	Kernel: Threads Over Time	Applications that are starting threads and not terminating them when the threads' tasks are completed. When the application itself is terminated, all threads will be terminated as well, but so long as the application is running unterminated, threads will continue to use up resources
	Memory Manager: Page-Outs	A shortage of physical memory leading to data being paged to disk even when still in use
	Memory Manager: Page Faults	Applications are calling for data that is no longer in memory but has been paged to disk. Some faults are normal, but a high number of page faults means slower performance (disk is slower than memory) and may indicate a need for more memory

T A B L E 5.2 *(cont.)*	**This Counter...**	**May Highlight This Problem...**
Troubleshooting with the System Monitor	Kernel: Processor Usage	If the user is not working but this value is still high, then some application may be running in the background, perhaps unbeknownst to the user
	Memory Manager: Locked Memory	If this value represents a large percentage of that shown by Allocated Memory, then only a limited amount of physical memory is available for new application needs. Data that is locked in memory cannot be paged to disk, so that physical memory is not released

Tuning and Optimizing the System

Windows 95's tools to tune the system include:

- A disk defragmenter

- A disk scanner

- An advanced compression utility

In order to work, both the disk defragger and scanner require volume locking to gain exclusive control of the volume being defragmented or scanned. Most applications use one, unexclusive set of calls to the file system driver to read and write to the disk, but these disk utilities use calls that bypass the file system driver and do not permit other applications to read or write to the disk until the application releases the volume.

Disk Geometry

To understand how Disk Defragmenter, ScanDisk, and the Compression Agent do their jobs, it's crucial to have some understanding of disk geometry.

Computer disks are divided physically into circles called *tracks* and in pie-shaped wedges radiating from their centers. The pieces created by the intersection of the concentric circles and the pie-shaped wedges are called *sectors*. Sectors are, in their turn, grouped logically into *clusters*. The number of sectors in a cluster will depend on the file system in use on the disk and the size of the disk.

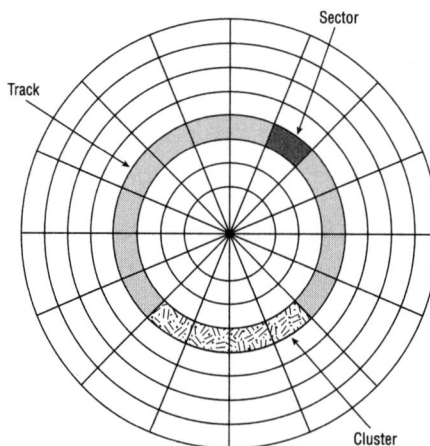

All other things being equal, the larger the disk partition, the larger the cluster size. Cluster size is relevant because data is stored (and retrieved) according to cluster; they're the smallest storage unit on the disk.

There's a tradeoff inherent in cluster size. Large clusters, used on large disk partitions, may lead to wasted space on the disk because small files will not use an entire cluster but the space will be unavailable to other files. Small clusters, on the other hand, increase the likelihood of file fragmentation and thus may increase data retrieval time.

Disk Defragmenter

As noted in the sidebar, data is stored in logical groups of sectors, known as clusters. When you're creating a new file, the clusters closest to the beginning of the disk are filled in first, logically enough. If a file is too big to fit completely into cluster 10, then clusters 11, 12, and 13 will be used up until the file is completely stored. When a disk is new and you're creating files, the clusters are filled up neatly and files are generally stored in consecutive clusters.

However, when you delete files or edit them, you may free up clusters. Data will still be stored in clusters as they are available, but those clusters may not all be consecutive now. Data may now be stored in clusters 10, 11, 45, and 116. This doesn't affect data integrity, but it does slow down retrieval time as the disk needle must move to different parts of the disk to retrieve the file.

That's what defragging is for. It doesn't free up space on your hard disk—a file that required four clusters before the defragging will use up four clusters after the defragging—but it will put all of a file's data in adjoining clusters.

Windows 95's defragger is located in the System Tools section of the Accessories folder. When you start it, it'll ask you which drive you want to defragment (see Figure 5.4).

FIGURE 5.4

Windows 95's defragger helps better organize your data.

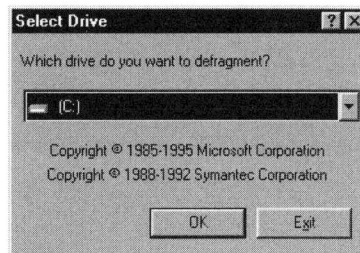

> For best results, don't run other programs while running the disk defragger. Although the defragger will still work, it will restart each time you write data to the disk.

Full defragmentation both consolidates free space and degfragments files. Choosing one of the other two options will probably be faster than performing a full defragmentation but won't accomplish as much. Choose a drive to defragment, and click OK. If you wish, you can watch the defragmenting process by clicking on the Details button (see Figure 5.5).

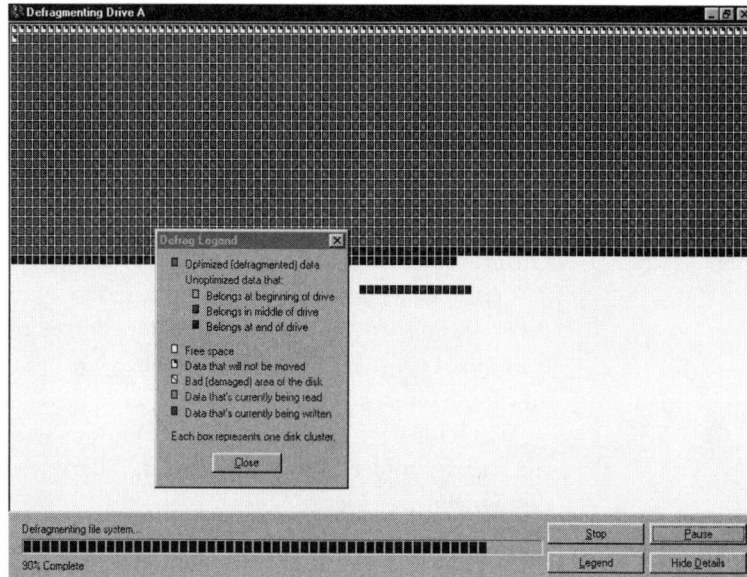

Displaying the details will slow down system performance.

Depending on how fragmented the drive was, you should see some improvement in data retrieval times once the process is complete.

ScanDisk

Clusters can get lost, which means that the file system can't find them to store data on them. The surface of a disk can also get damaged. Windows 95 comes with a utility that can diagnose these problems for both hard disks and floppy disks. Although ScanDisk can't fix physical damage to a disk, it can find lost clusters and mark areas of the hard disk as unusable so that the file system doesn't attempt to write data there that might prove unreadable.

ScanDisk comes in two versions: a graphical one and a text-based one. The graphical version is installed with Windows, whereas the text-based version is stored on the Startup disk. You can use the text-based one in batch files, scheduling events even without MS Plus installed.

ScanDisk is located in the System Tools section of the Accessories folder. When you initialize it, you'll need to select the drive you want to check for errors (see Figure 5.6).

FIGURE 5.6

Use ScanDisk to diagnose and repair disk errors.

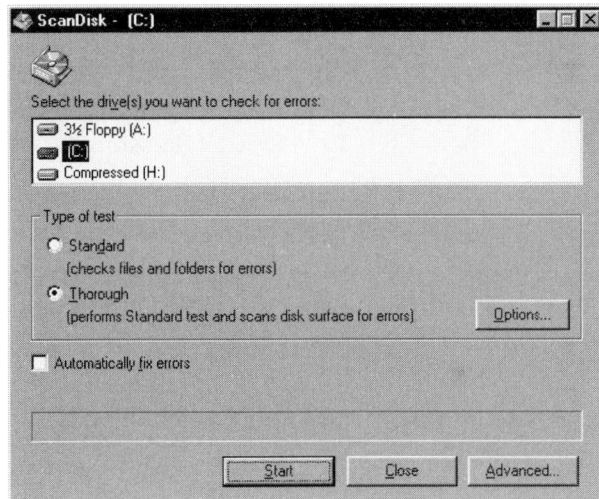

To run ScanDisk, choose a drive to repair and the options you want. Clicking on the Options button will let you further refine the scan, letting you choose the areas of the disk to be scanned and the type of testing to be done (see Figure 5.7).

When you click OK, the scanning process will begin. This will take a while, and unless you've chosen to let Windows 95 automatically fix errors it encounters, you'll have to manually decide what to do about each error that ScanDisk encounters.

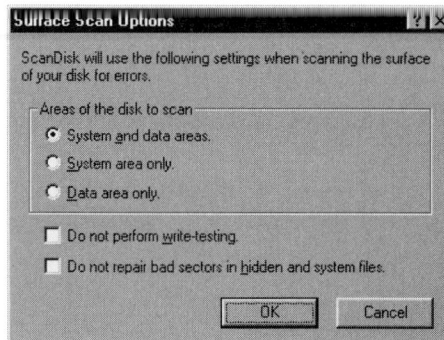

Compression Agent

Unit 3 discussed the options available with the Windows 95 native compression utility, DriveSpace. Microsoft Plus offers a few more compression options in its Compression Agent.

- Unlike DriveSpace, which compresses an entire volume, the Compression Agent permits you to compress individual files and folders.

- Compression Agent also compresses files when no other work is being done on the computer.

- Compression Agent can compress drives up to 2GB in size, whereas DriveSpace is limited to 512MB drives.

Compression Agent gives you the option of compressing rarely used files, based on the Last Accessed date of those files.

Compression Agent can also compress data further than can DriveSpace, compressing data in 32KB blocks instead of the 8KB blocks used by the standard Windows 95 compression utility. It comes with two forms of compression:

- HiPack, which uses the same format as DriveSpace but searches the entire history buffer for matches, not just a history window

- UltraPack, which uses a different encoding format but offers a higher degree of compression

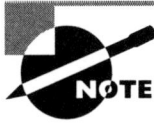

The more compressed files are, the longer it takes to read them from disk.

As HiPack uses the same format as DriveSpace, you can read HiPack volumes on a Windows 95 computer that does not have Microsoft Plus installed. UltraPack volumes may only be read from a computer that does have Microsoft Plus and the Compression Agent installed.

Microsoft Plus comes with a timer called System Agent, which you can use to automatically run Compression Agent (and other disk utilities) at certain times.

Disk compression is a trade-off between the increased disk space garnered and the performance hit incurred by the time required to compress and decompress files. Table 5.3 outlines how you can use Compression Agent to best meet your needs.

T A B L E 5.3 Fine-Tuning Compression Agent	To achieve...	Then...
	Maximum disk space	Use UltraPack compression, and compress files as they are saved
	Best system performance	Only compress files during off-hours, or when system is low. Only compress files not used for a long time. Don't compress executable files
	Maximum flexibility	Use HiPack compression so removable disks may be read at computers that don't have Microsoft Plus installed

STUDY QUESTIONS

Monitoring System Performance

1. When peer-to-peer services are enabled, what utility can you use to review the folders and files that are being shared and who is accessing them?

   _____

2. List two parameters in System Monitor that if exhibiting high activity might indicate a need for more physical memory.

   _____

   _____

3. What tool can be used to evaluate performance of subsystems to identify problems and possibly justify hardware upgrades?

   _____

4. True or False: System Monitor allows you to monitor TCP/IP activity.

5. True or False: Windows 95 includes tools to view information provided by the Network Monitor Agent.

6. True or False: NetWatcher allows you to remotely create shares on a PC.

7. Which options must you select from the menu bar to share a folder using NetWatcher?

   _____

8.   Using NetWatcher, how can you stop the sharing of a particular folder?

_____

9.   By default, only those with _____ privileges may use tools that call for Remote Registry services.

10.   A _____ is the smallest unit of an application or operating system.

11.   True or False: To keep track of the swap file size, you should monitor the File System object.

12.   What is the relationship between the Memory Manager counters for Page Outs and Page Faults?

_____

_____

_____

13.   Bytes read and written per second is recorded in the _____ category(ies).

14.   True or False: You can potentially have multiple counters for dropped packets.

15. Windows NT uses a tool called the Network Monitor to keep an eye on network traffic, including broadcast frames transmitted per second. Explain how you would keep track of this data from a Windows 95 machine.

_____

_____

_____

16. True or False: Page faults are always undesirable.

17. Which System Monitor counter keeps track of disk usage, specifically remaining disk space?

_____

_____

Tuning and Optimizing the System

18. A user wants to schedule programs to run automatically, and not only at startup. What Microsoft product does the user need?

_____

19. True or False: The DriveSpace feature included with Windows 95 allows for a maximum compressed drive size of 512MB.

20. What utility can you use to check and correct problems with the directory tree structure?

_____

21. List the areas of a disk the ScanDisk checks.

22. Is there any difference between the cluster sizes used with the DriveSpace supplied with Windows 95, and that which is supplied with Microsoft Plus? If so, what is the difference?

23. Why use the Compression Agent over DriveSpace?

24. How do you determine the most accurate compression estimate?

25. Which file can be compressed more, a program file or a bitmap file?

26. When a drive is being defragmented, you are provided with a small status window that assesses the progress. What are the three buttons provided in this window?

_____

_____

_____

27. True or False: By default, the Windows 95 Disk Defragmenter does not check for disk errors when it is run.

28. Name the three defragmentation methods that are made available to you.

_____

_____

_____

29. To defragment a drive, right-click on its icon within the My Computer folder and select _____. Then, from the window presented, select the _____ tab and then Defragment Now.

30. Name the two compression methods offered by the Microsoft Plus compression agent.

_____

_____

31. To ensure that lost clusters are not wasting valuable disk space, what utility should be run?

_____

32. What feature in Windows 95 allows for utilities such as ScanDisk and Defrag to be run from within Windows?

_____

33. True or False: Defragmenting your hard disk will create more space on it.

34. How can you see defragmentation information for a drive?

_____

35. Why shouldn't you run other programs while using the Disk Defragmenter?

36. When a drive is compressed, you will usually gain between _____ and 100 percent more space.

37. True or False: If you install Microsoft Plus, the System Agent will automatically schedule ScanDisk to run.

38. How many versions of ScanDisk does Windows 95 ship with?

_____

39. True or False: Running Defrag with the full details option does not incur a performance penalty.

40. What should you do to ensure that the Disk Defragmenter runs as quickly as possible?

_____

41. True or False: ScanDisk works with the file system driver to gain exclusive access to the disk.

42. The smallest physical unit on a disk is called a(n) _____.

43. What is the purpose of volume locking?

_____

_____

SAMPLE TEST

5-1   From the Disk Defragmenter window, what action do you take to override Defrag's default optimization choice?

   A. Click the Choices button.

   B. Click the Options button.

   C. Click the Advanced button.

   D. Click the Change button.

5-2   Data is stored on disk in logical units called:

   A. Tracks

   B. Clusters

   C. Sectors

   D. Wedges

5-3   Which of the following are features of Compression Agent but are not found in DriveSpace? Choose all that apply.

   A. Compression of drives up to 4GB in size

   B. Compression of individual files and folders within a volume

   C. Taking space from a drive and creating a separate compressed volume

   D. Automatic compression of files that have not been accessed for a predetermined period of time

5-4 Which of the following would be indicated by a high and increasing value for Kernel: Threads Over Time? Choose all that apply.

    A. A large number of applications running simultaneously

    B. A need for a faster processor

    C. An application that does not terminate its threads properly

    D. None of the above

5-5 Which of the following statements about the NetWatcher are not true? Choose all that apply.

    A. If you're running NetWatcher on a computer using user-level security, you'll only be able to monitor other computers using user-level security.

    B. When running NetWatcher on NetWare networks, you will not be able to disconnect users from resources, but you will be able to close files that those users are accessing.

    C. Computers to be monitored must be running both the Remote Registry Services and File and Print Services.

    D. None of the above.

5-6 By default, which users have the right to access computers running the Remote Registry Service from across the network? Choose all that apply.

    A. Administrators

    B. The local user

    C. Power users

    D. All users

5-7   You're working on a fast laptop with limited hard disk space. The laptop is the only computer on the network with Microsoft Plus installed. Which compression type would be most useful to you, and why?

   A. UltraPack, compressing all files as they're created and edited

   B. HiPack, compressing all files as they're created and edited

   C. UltraPack, compressing only files older than a certain date

   D. None of the above

5-8   Which of the following is not a System Monitor category? Choose all that apply. (The wording used here may not be precisely the wording used in the category label.)

   A. Client for Microsoft Networks

   B. Memory Manager

   C. Evaluation of the Ethernet network

   D. NetBEUI monitoring

5-9   Which of the following categories monitors activity of the File and Print Sharing service?

   A. Microsoft Network Monitor

   B. Microsoft Network Server

   C. Microsoft Network Client

   D. Microsoft Client for NetWare Networks

5-10   Which of the following may be counted with the System Monitor if you choose the IPX/SPX-Compatible counter? Choose all that apply.

   A. SAP advertisements

   B. Bytes read and written per second

   C. Dropped packets

   D. Free sockets

5-11   You're concerned about whether your machine has sufficient physical memory to meet your usage patterns. Which of the following System Monitor counters could provide you with useful information to help you determine this? Choose all that apply.

   A. Memory Manager: Page Faults

   B. Memory Manager: Page Outs

   C. Memory Manager: Locked Memory

   D. None of the above

5-12   What will happen if you run an application that's stored on the disk you're trying to defragment?

   A. The defragger will fail.

   B. The application will fail.

   C. You will be able to run the application, but will have to store data to a different drive.

   D. The defragger will restart each time the application writes data to the disk.

5-13   To improve disk access times, you should run:

   A. The defragging utility

   B. ScanDisk

   C. System Monitor

   D. MEM /P

UNIT

6

Troubleshooting

Test Objectives: Troubleshooting

■ Diagnose and resolve installation failures.

■ Diagnose and resolve boot process failures.

■ Diagnose and resolve connectivity problems in a Microsoft environment and a mixed Microsoft and NetWare environment. Tools include:

- WinIPCfg
- NetWatcher
- Troubleshooting wizards

■ Diagnose and resolve printing problems in a Microsoft environment and a mixed Microsoft and NetWare environment.

■ Diagnose and resolve file system problems.

■ Diagnose and resolve resource access problems in a Microsoft environment and a mixed Microsoft and NetWare environment.

■ Diagnose and resolve hardware device and device driver problems. Tools include:

- MSD
- Add/Remove Hardware Wizard

■ Perform direct modification of the Registry as appropriate by using REGEDIT.

NOTE Exam objectives are subject to change at any time without prior notice and at Microsoft's sole discretion. Please visit Microsoft's Training & Certification Web site (www.microsoft.com/Train_Cert/) for the most current listing of exam objectives.

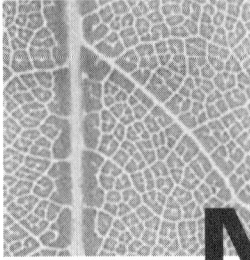

No matter how well set up an operating system may be, some troubleshooting will almost certainly be required some day. This unit reviews methods of troubleshooting every aspect of Windows 95.

Installation Failures

Windows 95 Setup has certain requirements:

- BIOS-based virus checking must be turned off.
- At least 420KB of conventional memory must be free.

To get enough conventional memory, make sure that DOS is loaded into the Upper Memory Area.

- Its hardware requirements must be met.
- HIMEM.SYS and EMM386.EXE must be loaded in CONFIG.SYS.
- The drive/network from which you're running Setup must be working properly.
- CONFIG.SYS and AUTOEXEC.BAT should be stripped of any commands not required to initialize the system or (when applicable) the network.
- If you're running a server-based Setup, the network connection and server logon must be functioning properly.

Setup Hangs

Press F3 or click the Exit button to terminate Setup. If that doesn't work, press Ctrl+Alt+Del, or, if need be, manually turn off the computer, wait a few seconds, and restart.

Setup should restart in Safe Recovery Mode and skip the part of Setup that caused the problem.

> The Hardware Detection portion of Setup must be completed, however. Keep restarting Setup until this portion is finished. If hardware detection repeatedly fails, make sure the hardware is compatible with Windows 95.

Setup Won't Start

If Setup won't start, you can:

- Run a virus-checker on the computer.

- Make sure that HIMEM.SYS and EMM386.EXE are loaded in CONFIG.SYS.

- Make sure enough conventional memory is available. DOS should be loaded in the UMA, and no TSRs should be loaded unless vital for operations.

Setup Fails When Running from Floppy Disk

If the Setup fails when you're using a floppy disk, you can:

- See whether the disk can be read in another machine, or whether another disk can be read in the drive.

- Disable any BIOS-based virus-checking routines.

- Check system documentation to be sure the drive CMOS settings are correct.

- Use DRIVEPARM to configure the floppy drive, if necessary.

Setup Fails When Running from CD

If it fails when you're using a CD, you can:

- See whether the CD can be read in another machine, or whether another CD can be read locally.

- Make sure that the CD drivers were loaded in AUTOEXEC.BAT.

- Check system documentation to be sure that the CD drive CMOS settings are correct.

You Cannot Access the Server during a Network-Based Installation

If you can't access the server while you're performing a network-based installation, you can:

- Make sure you have an account on that server and that your account is being validated properly—you'll need the proper password and user rights.

- Make sure the network itself is working.

- Make sure enough conventional memory is free.

- Make sure any login scripts are working.

The Network Connection Fails during Installation

If your network connection fails during installation, you can:

- Attempt to reconnect to the server.

- Make sure the network itself is working—check for loose connectors and breaks in the line.

- Test the connection from another machine.

- Reboot your computer and attempt to reconnect to the server.

Setup Freezes during Hardware Detection

If the computer freezes during hardware detection, you can:

- Be sure that it's really hanging—some detection routines can take several minutes to work.

- If the system isn't responding after five minutes, then reboot.

- To disable hardware detection for a certain class of devices, choose to define your own installed hardware during Setup, and make sure the problem components are not checked.

Setup Fails with a B1 Error

This error indicates your system's CPU is an old 80386 processor and needs to be upgraded. Windows 95 will not work with this CPU.

Computer Stalls after Copying All Files

May indicate that BIOS-based virus-checking software was still running. Reboot, disable the virus checker, and run Setup in Safe Recovery Mode.

You Get an "Incorrect DOS Version" Message

If you're running a version of DOS prior to 3.1, this means you need to upgrade first—Windows 95 cannot be installed over older versions of DOS.

If your version of DOS is recent, but you see this message, the problem may lie in DOS memory management software 386MAX. Disable the memory manager and rerun Setup.

You See a "Standard Mode: Error in DOS Extender" Message

You may see this message when running Setup from within DOS. It indicates a memory conflict in the Upper Memory Area. To resolve it, either disable upper-memory blocks with the line

```
DOS=HIGH, no UMB
```

in `CONFIG.SYS` or remove `EMM386` from `CONFIG.SYS`. Alternatively, run Setup from Windows.

You Can't Open an *.INF* File

You may have run out of conventional memory. Make sure that all applications are closed and no TSRs are running.

Setup Is Unable to Find a Valid Boot Partition

Windows 95 must be able to find a valid boot partition in order to run:

- Make sure the drive is not mapped over or logically remapped.
- Run FDISK to make sure that a valid boot partition exists, and create one if necessary.
- Remove any driver files interfering with the boot partition and rerun Setup.
- If you're using disk compression software, make sure that the assigned letters don't conflict with the letter of the boot drive.

Setup Can't Find Sufficient Free Space

Setup needs about 35–45MB of disk space on the drive. If this is not available, exit Setup and find out how much disk space is available.

You Can't Run OS/2 after Completing Setup

Setup disables the OS/2 Boot Manager. You'll need to enable it again after installing Windows 95, using the OS/2 boot disk and the OS/2 version of FDISK.

> **NOTE** If you run DOS from a floppy disk and then run Setup, you will not be able to run OS/2 afterward. To avoid this, rename the OS/2 CONFIG.SYS and AUTOEXEC.BAT files before running Setup so they don't get overwritten.

An Automated Installation from *MSBATCH.INF* Fails

If this happens, you can:

- Make sure the network is running.

- Check command syntax within the .INF file.
- Review any error messages.
- Make sure sufficient conventional memory is available.
- Make sure the client is properly authenticated on the server.

Boot Process Failures

Generally speaking, if Windows 95 experiences minor startup problems related to system configuration (such as a video driver that doesn't work), it will start in Safe Mode. More serious problems may require other responses, however.

Windows 95 Stalls during the First Reboot after Installation

Generally, this happens because some hardware was incorrectly configured before installation of Windows 95. Boot with a stripped-down version of your AUTOEXEC.BAT and CONFIG.SYS files in order to identify the problem component, and then set it up properly. Also, make sure all SCSI chains are properly terminated—particularly if your hard disk is SCSI. SCSI chains must be terminated on both ends.

It's possible you may have to disable the ISA enumerator, a piece of software that detects a new adapter type that can be configured from the operating system. The ISA enumerator references ports not commonly in use, but which may be used by other hardware.

To disable the ISA enumerator, remove or comment out the following line from SYSTEM.INI: device=isapnp.386.

You Get a "Bad or Missing *File Name*" Message

If Windows 95 can't detect a valid copy of HIMEM.SYS, IFSHELP.SYS, or other key system files required to run the operating system, it will complain about it. The file must be uncorrupted, in the proper location, and of the most recent vintage available.

> If you have a working machine around, you may be able to copy the missing/corrupted file from that machine to the one that isn't working.

If you're loading a driver that's necessary for the system to read your hard disk, be sure to place that driver at the beginning of CONFIG.SYS so that Windows 95 can read the drive and load the operating system files.

If a crucial Windows 95 file is missing, you'll need to rerun Setup in Safe Recovery Mode.

The *SYSTEM.DAT* Registry File Is Missing

If only SYSTEM.DAT is missing, then the problem probably isn't severe—each time Windows 95 boots successfully, a copy of SYSTEM.DAT is saved as SYSTEM.DA0 and saves all the Registry settings found therein. If SYSTEM.DAT is damaged between reboots, then SYSTEM.DA0 is loaded in its place. Any changes to the Registry during the last session will be lost, but the system will boot.

If SYSTEM.DA0 is also lost, however, then you won't have this option. No Registry services will run, which for all practical purposes means that the operating system won't run. You'll either have to restore SYSTEM.DAT from backups or rerun Setup and return to a vanilla configuration.

> Keep a backup copy of your system's SYSTEM.DAT around to restore in case of an emergency, and update it regularly. You don't even have to use the text-based Registry Editor to restore it—just copy it to the root directory of the boot drive.

Windows 95 Stalls While Starting

One possible cause of system stalls and failed installations is BIOS-based virus protection software, which prevents Windows 95 from overwriting the boot sector. If Windows 95 does not start normally, inspect your computer's CMOS settings and turn off virus protection if it's enabled. Then reinstall Windows 95.

The Computer Is Not Starting Due to Missing Real-Mode Drivers

Another operating system may have trouble starting if certain real-mode drivers on which it depends aren't loaded properly.

To determine which real-mode drivers are damaged or missing, press F8 when the Starting Windows 95 message appears and choose Step-By-Step confirmation to watch all drivers being loaded. If a driver does not appear, make sure that it's named in the appropriate startup file and in the proper path.

A Virtual Device Driver Is Damaged or Missing

If a virtual device driver (VxD) is not functioning properly, you'll see an error message. If the driver is crucial to the functioning of Windows 95, then the operating system will not start and you'll be left at the command prompt. To replace the missing VxD, run Setup and choose Verify or Safe Recovery.

Windows 95 Starts Automatically, Not Giving You the Option to Choose Another Operating System

To boot to another operating system, you must set the value of BootMulti equal to 1 in MSDOS.SYS (editable with a text editor such as Notepad). Windows 95 will not dual-boot with versions of DOS older than 5, or with DR-DOS. You cannot boot to a previous version of Windows if you installed Windows 95 into the same directory and overwrote the previous version.

If the problem is that you're getting a "Previous DOS files not found" message, the most likely cause is that you're trying to dual-boot to a version of DOS prior to 5.0. The only way that you can do this is to boot from floppy disk.

Connectivity Failures

Windows 95 comes with three tools to help you diagnose connectivity problems:

- WinIPCfg
- NetWatcher
- Troubleshooting wizards

WinIPCfg

If you're using IP address leasing on your network in an effort to cut down on administrative work, your IP address will change from time to time. WinIPCfg is an undocumented tool with which you can determine your current IP address—the only Windows 95 tool, in fact.

`WINIPCFG.EXE` is located in your Windows 95 directory. When you run it, you'll see the IP Configuration dialog box (see Figure 6.1).

FIGURE 6.1

Getting IP information with WinIPCFG

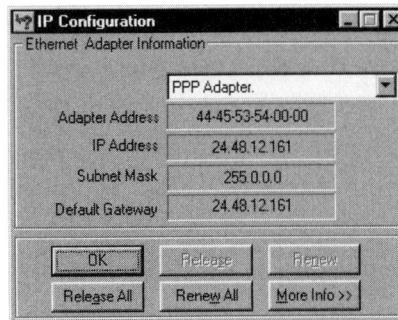

Essentially, this tool is good for getting a snapshot of your IP connection: the subnet mask, the address of your default gateway and any DNS servers and WINS servers as applicable, and the date of your lease. You can't change any of the IP configuring information with this tool, but you can either give up or renew your IP leasing, and you can see in one easy-to-access dialog box whether all the addresses are set as they should be. Use the More Info button to see more information, such as DNS and WINS servers. You can also look at multiple adapters by using the drop-down box for the adapter.

WARNING Do not renew or release your IP address without permission from the network administrator.

NetWatcher

If you're having trouble connecting to a resource and you have the proper permissions, you can run NetWatcher on the remote computer to see the status of shared resources, including the following:

- What files and resources are shared

- Who's connected to them

- What files are open

For example, running NetWatcher can tell you the share name of a resource has been changed, or a formerly shared resource is no longer available.

To run NetWatcher on a computer, the following must be true:

- The computer must be running the Remote Registry services.

- You must have the proper rights to access the computer (by default, this means only members of the Administrators group on computers with user-level security enabled).

- You must either be running user-level security on your computer or be connecting to a computer using share-level security

Troubleshooting Wizards

Windows 95 includes some premade scripts to help you troubleshoot common problems. Run Windows 95 Help (on the Start menu), and look up the word "troubleshooting" in the Index. In the list of subtopics, select "connection problems." You'll see a dialog box like the one shown in Figure 6.2.

When you choose a topic, Windows 95 will walk you through the situation, asking questions (as shown in Figure 6.3) and suggesting solutions based on your replies.

FIGURE 6.2

Using Help wizards to solve connection problems

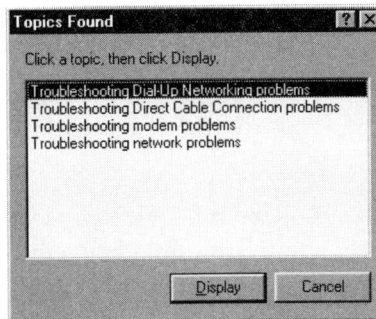

Topics Found

Click a topic, then click Display.

Troubleshooting Dial-Up Networking problems
Troubleshooting Direct Cable Connection problems
Troubleshooting modem problems
Troubleshooting network problems

Display   Cancel

FIGURE 6.3

Walking through a problem with a connection Help wizard

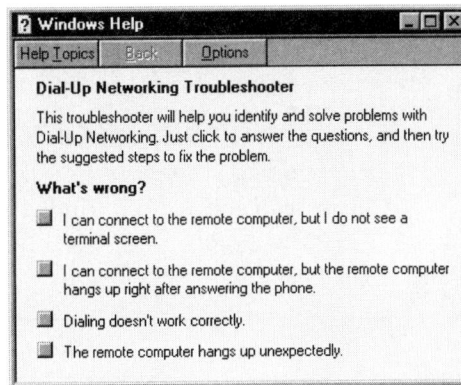

Windows Help

Help Topics   Back   Options

Dial-Up Networking Troubleshooter

This troubleshooter will help you identify and solve problems with Dial-Up Networking. Just click to answer the questions, and then try the suggested steps to fix the problem.

What's wrong?

☐ I can connect to the remote computer, but I do not see a terminal screen.

☐ I can connect to the remote computer, but the remote computer hangs up right after answering the phone.

☐ Dialing doesn't work correctly.

☐ The remote computer hangs up unexpectedly.

The Help wizards cover a general list of troubleshooting topics, not just connectivity problems.

Printer Problems

Printer problems may be divided into two categories:

- Problems with installing the printer
- Problems with printing to the printer

Installation Problems

You may run into problems installing a printer if:

- The printer's .INF file does not exist or is not stored in the INF directory of the Windows folder. Verify the .INF file's existence and location.

- Setup is unable to find the printer driver files. By default, Setup will check the installation directory for the files, but if it can't find them it will prompt you for the correct path. You may need the Windows 95 disks or CD to supply the files.

- You experience an error while copying the files from the source directory. If so, verify that you've specified the right source location for the files, and that the disk/CD/network is available.

Printing Problems

Not all printing problems are created equal. See Table 6.1 if you can't print at all, or see Table 6.2 for printing output that looks weird.

T A B L E 6.1: You Can't Print At All

Possible Cause	Diagnosis	Solution/Resolution
You may have sent a print job to the wrong printer	Make sure you're printing to the printer you think you are	Right-click on the installed printers in the Printers folder to see which is the default printer (it will have a check mark next to the Set as Default item in the pop-up menu). One printer will always be the default
The print job may not yet have been spooled to the printer	Make sure that the print job isn't still processing. A large job may take a while to spool, or other jobs may be ahead of your's	Double-click on the printer's icon to see a list of pending print jobs. If no jobs are queued, then turn the printer off and back on again to clear its buffer, and resend the job
You may not be connected to the printer	If you're on a network, the network connection may have failed. Any printer may be unplugged or offline	Make sure that the printer is plugged into the computer and online. Test the network connection. Print a test page from the printer's Properties sheet

T A B L E 6.1: You Can't Print At All *(continued)*

Possible Cause	Diagnosis	Solution/Resolution
You can't send a print job to the printer	You may be out of disk space on the drive that holds the temporary files	Check available disk space, and run ScanDisk. Delete old .EMF temp files and spool files (.SPL), found in the TEMP directory and in SYSTEM\ SPOOL\PRINTERS, respectively.
Printing is slower than normal	Could have several causes, including memory issues, hard disk space restrictions, and demands on system resources	Defragment the printer server's hard disk. Check system resources. Try printing in Safe Mode-Make sure that EMF spooling is enabled. Disable Print True Types as Graphics, if enabled. Make sure that the proper printer driver is loaded, and reinstall it if necessary
You can't print to a printer connected to a non-Microsoft server	You may need to redirect the port to the shared printer	Redirect the port to the shared printer path, and rerun the Add Printer Wizard to set up the printer to use that port

T A B L E 6.2: Output is Garbled, Incomplete, or Looks Funny

Situation	Diagnosis	Solution/Resolution
Your print jobs are full of garbage that has nothing to do with the print job you sent out	You may be using the wrong printer driver	Check the driver, as shown in the printer's Properties sheet. Print a test page from the General tab in the Properties sheet. If this doesn't work, try setting the driver to Generic/Text only or Generic Laser Printer Driver. Also, make sure that the printer driver's description in the Registry is accurate
Formatting information for the print job is lost or corrupted, or images are half-printed or missing	You may be experiencing memory overruns, or trouble printing from an application	Disable EMF spooling Reduce print resolution Print a test page to make sure the printer works Try to print in Safe Mode
The printer is printing only part of a page	May be memory overruns, or a problem printing from that application	Try reducing document complexity, including the number of fonts and lines in the document Try printing the document from another application, or changing the document's fonts Enable Print TrueType as Graphics to reduce memory needs

Generally speaking, try the following:

- To see whether Windows 95 and the printer are communicating properly, print a test page.

- Simplify print jobs if long or complex jobs are not printing properly, or send jobs directly to the printer without spooling.

- Turn the printer off and back on to clear its buffer.

- Make sure that the printer is plugged in and online and has paper and ink.

- Try to print to a file. If you can do so, copy the file to the printer's port with the `copy /b filename lptx` command, where *filename* is the name of the file and *lptx* is the name of the port the printer's connected to. If this works, then Windows 95 is having a problem communicating with the printer.

- Make sure you can connect to the network print server.

- If a printer driver does not work, try using the generic drivers or printing from DOS to determine whether the Windows 95 driver is corrupt.

- For PostScript printers with memory problems, print in raster-graphics mode instead of vector-graphics mode, which takes up more memory.

- If you suspect you can't print because of a bi-directional printing problem, disable bi-directional printing in the printer's Properties sheet (in the Spool Settings section of Details). If printing now works, make sure you have a 1284-compliant printer cable.

File System Problems

Some of the problems you're likely to encounter with file systems come from using utilities not intended for use with Windows 95 (see Table 6.3).

T A B L E 6.3:   Diagnosing File System Problems Caused by Software Incompatibilities

Problem	Possible Diagnosis/Solution
A disk utility won't work	Unless the disk utility is designed for use with Windows 95's file system, it may not work. Use a utility designed for Windows 95 instead
Your shortcuts no longer work after compressing your Windows 95 volume with Stacker	Stacker does not recognize long file names, so the shortcuts will be to the aliases, not to the filenames to which they were originally built. You will need to redefine your shortcuts. You will also need to move USER.DAT and USER.DA0 from the host volume to the compressed drive
Virus-cleaning utilities detect, but do not remove, viruses	Virus cleaners designed for Windows will not remove viruses from a Windows 95 volume. You can successfully run DOS-based virus checkers, however
A file's alias was changed when the file was copied to a new directory	If you used a DOS-based command such as Copy to copy the file, the alias will not go with the long file name and a new alias will be created
A long filename was destroyed	Often caused by running a backup utility not intended for use with Windows 95, or when a file is copied to an operating system that does not support long file names. (Editing a file in an application that does not support long file names will not affect the file name, so long as the application is running on Windows 95.) You can back up long file names with the Windows 95 utility LFNBK
The /mount command in AUTOEXEC.BAT used to mount volumes compressed with DriveSpace or DoubleSpace no longer works.	Windows 95 deletes or renames any versions of DriveSpace or DoubleSpace it finds in its directory. Replace the program information in AUTOEXEC.BAT with SCANDISK

Other problems are part of Windows 95's design (see Table 6.4).

T A B L E 6.4: Diagnosing File System Problems That Are Part of Windows' Design

Problem	Possible Diagnosis/Solution
Windows 95 reports 2GB free space on a network-accessible drive, with no bytes used	For compatibility reasons, older versions of Windows 95 were not designed to work with disks larger than 2GB. If accessing a larger volume, Windows 95 may report erroneous volume sizes and free space. Microsoft does not recommend using Windows 95 with volumes larger than 2GB
A compressed volume file will not mount	Check the DBLSPACE.INI file in the root directory of the boot drive. If this file is corrupted, then you'll need to recreate it with DoubleSpace
Disk device drivers cause the system to stall at boot time	Disk device drivers must be located in the SYSTEM\IOSUBSYS directory of the Windows 95 folder. Replace all real-mode disk drivers with protected-mode drivers if possible, looking in IOSYS.INI to determine which need to be replaced

To configure file system settings, turn to the Performance tab of the System applet (found in the Control Panel) and click on File System settings. The Hard Disk tab allows you to specify the computer's usual role, to best optimize disk caching. Your options are outlined in Table 6.5.

T A B L E 6.5: Computer Roles and Their File Caching settings

Role	File Caching Settings
Desktop Computer (the default)	Intended for stand-alone machines and network clients with adequate memory for their needs. Caches the 32 most recently accessed folders and 677 most recently used files. This setting uses 10KB of memory
Mobile or Docking System	Intended for mobile computers, or any computer with minimal memory resources. Caches the 16 most recently accessed folders and 337 most recently used files. This setting uses 5KB of memory
Network Server	Intended for systems acting as file or print servers, ones that get a lot of disk access. Caches the 40 most recently accessed folders and 2,729 most recently used files. This setting uses 40KB of memory

Adjusting your computer's role can help you get more use from existing memory and cache space. Caching more files than is necessary will use memory that could have been used elsewhere, but caching fewer files than necessary will slow down file access.

Generally speaking, Windows 95 is optimized for high-speed disk access and file caching. If you're experiencing problems with the file system, you can try disabling some of the file-caching features, noting that doing so will likely impact performance. Disable these features from the Troubleshooting tab of the File System Properties sheet (see Figure 6.4).

F I G U R E 6.4

Troubleshooting
options for disk access

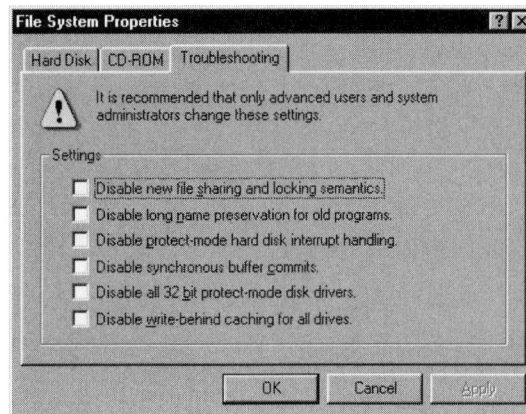

These options and the problems to which they relate are described in Table 6.6.

T A B L E 6.6:   Results of Using Disk Access Troubleshooting Options

Problem	Disable	Result
A DOS application has problems with sharing files under Windows 95	New File Sharing and Locking Semantics	Changes the rules that govern how files may be shared without being modified by two applications at once
A legacy application can't open files with long file names, even using the alias	Long File Name Preservation for Old Programs	Turns off tunneling, the option that preserves long file names even when a file is opened in a DOS or Win16 application

T A B L E 6.6: Results of Using Disk Access Troubleshooting Options *(continued)*

Problem	Disable	Result
The hard disk is not processing interrupts properly	Protected-Mode Hard Disk Interrupt Handling	Makes ROM routines handle all interrupts, instead of Windows 95, which is faster
The computer won't boot because of disk I/O problems	32-Bit Protected Mode Drivers	Only real-mode disk drivers will be used, which will disable any disks dependent on the protected-mode drivers
You need to make sure that all data is written *immediately* to disk, not cached and flushed in chunks	Write-Behind Caching for All Drives	Writes all data to disk as it's saved. This will reduce performance

Resource Access Problems

Generally speaking, problems with connecting to network resources fall into one of three categories:

- Use of incompatible network protocols or frame type
- Not having the proper rights and permissions to access the desired resources
- Hardware or software-related network problems

Protocol Issues

To connect to any network resource, you must be using the same transport protocol as its server: Connecting to the Internet requires TCP/IP, connecting to NetWare servers requires IPX/SPX-compatible protocol, and so forth. Even within protocols, you must do some checking:

- For IPX/SPX networks, make sure you're using the right frame type. Versions 3.1 and earlier of NetWare use 802.3 and versions 3.12 and 4.x use 802.2. Normally, Windows 95 automatically detects the proper frame type needed, but if it doesn't, you need to find out which version of NetWare you're connecting to, and manually set the proper frame type from the IPX/SPX-compatible protocol settings in the Network applet.

- For TCP/IP networks, make sure that all your addresses are correct: DHCP server, WINS server, default gateway, and so forth.

If your network is subnetted, the address of your default gateway or any other host on your subnet should look similar to your own. *How* similar will depend on the network class. If a Class C network, then the first three quads of the address should match yours. If a Class B, then only the first two will necessarily match.

Rights and Permissions

Having access to a resource does not always mean that you have full access to that resource. If a resource is shared with share-level security, then passwords may be assigned to give some users read-only access and some full access, and some no access at all. A resource shared from a system using user-level access has even more discretion when it comes to determining access type. Before assuming that something is wrong with the connection, find out what kind of access you've been given.

If you can't see a resource that you know is shared, find out whether it's been made a hidden share for added security. Naming a shared folder or printer with a dollar sign at the end of the name prevents that resource from showing up on a browse list.

Network Problems

Even if you are using the proper protocol and have the appropriate permissions to access a resource, you may run into problems if something is wrong with the network. For example, if you can't access a host on a TCP/IP network, follow this series of steps to find out which part of the network is not working:

1. Ping yourself with the loopback address: 127.0.0.1. If this ping works, then your network adapter is working properly.

2. Ping a known location on the local network, such as the default gateway. If your network is using DHCP to assign IP addresses, be sure to ping a stable location.

3. Ping a known location on another subnet, if applicable.

4. Ping a known location on the Internet, by name (such as `ibm.com`) or by number, If the name doesn't work.

Device and Device Driver Problems

Windows 95 may not recognize a device for one of three reasons:

- The device may not be properly connected.
- The device may not be using the correct driver.
- The device may conflict with another device's IRQ or I/O buffers.

You can diagnose most device problems with the Device Manager found in the System applet in the Control Panel (see Figure 6.5).

FIGURE 6.5

The Device Manager helps you troubleshoot device problems.

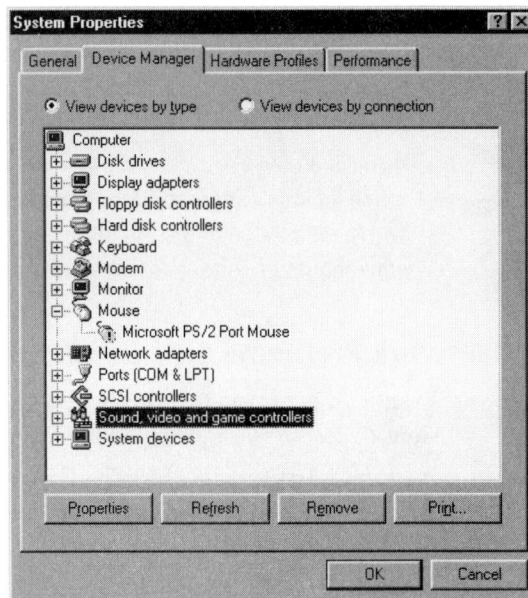

A device with an exclamation point next to it, as shown in Figure 6.5, isn't working properly. To diagnose the problem, select the device in the list and open its Properties sheet (see Figure 6.6). From here, you can determine which driver is in use (and replace it, if necessary), and check for resource conflicts.

FIGURE 6.6

Properties sheet for a
mouse that is not work-
ing properly

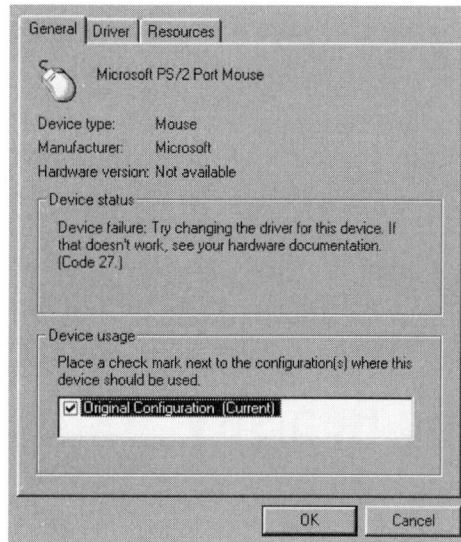

The Device Manager uses visual codes to help you see problems at a glance. For example, a resource conflict is indicated with an asterisk, whereas a device disabled for a particular hardware configuration is indicated with an X through it.

Using Microsoft System Diagnostics (MSD)

If you installed Windows 95 into its own directory, you'll retain MSD on your system. MSD is the pre-95 answer to the Device Manager, providing you with current configuration information about your computer's status. To run it, use the Run applet in the Start menu and type **msd**.

Once you run it, you'll see a DOS GUI menu of all system settings: memory, IRQs, disk space and type, and so forth. In some ways, MSD is much more comprehensive than the Device Manager—MSD shows you what TSRs are running and how much memory they're using, what your drive type is (useful if you're writing down system parameters and don't want to reboot), what IRQs are in use and for what, and so forth. Much of this information is organized in a manner that makes it easier to troubleshoot than Device Manager does. For example, if you suspect an IRQ conflict, you need to track down which devices are using which IRQs with

Device Manager. With MSD, you can look at a list of all system IRQs and see how they're allocated. The only catch to MSD is that it's only good for the virtual machine in which it's running. Microsoft recommends running MSD from DOS to get a more accurate picture of resource allocations.

> **NOTE** Although the Microsoft outline at the Training Certification site presently includes a reference to the Add/Remove Hardware Wizard, it's assumed that this is an error as no such wizard exists. There is an Add Hardware Wizard, and it's covered in Unit 2.

Editing the Registry

You should be able to do most troubleshooting from within the Control Panel and with other GUI tools, but now and then you need to edit it directly using REGEDIT, the Windows 95 Registry Editor.

The Registry is made up of six keys:

- HKEY_LOCAL_MACHINE
- HKEY_CURRENT_USER
- HKEY_DYN_DATA
- HKEY_USERS
- HKEY_CLASSES_ROOT
- HKEY_CURRENT_CONFIG

The key that you're most likely to edit is HKEY_LOCAL_MACHINE, which contains all machine-specific settings (see Figure 6.7).

To find a value in the Registry, press F3 to open the Find tool, or choose Edit ➤ Find. You may have to look at a few instances of a word before finding the one that corresponds to your needs. Press F3 to keep cycling through instances of the word.

F I G U R E 6.7

Contents of
HKEY_LOCAL_MACHINE

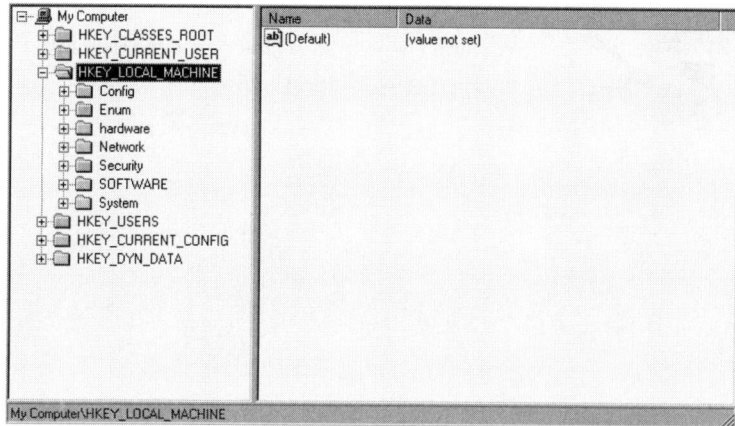

F I G U R E 6.7

Contents of
HKEY_LOCAL_MACHINE

Before editing the Registry, it's a good idea to back up all or part of it. You can do this from within the Registry Editor by choosing to Export the Registry, or a specific key. This exported file will be saved with a .REG extension. Do *not* run .REG files from within Explorer or My Computer unless you're sure that you want to replace the key they represent with their contents, as doing so will import them to the Registry.

Once you find the value to edit, double-click on it to change its value (see Figure 6.8). In this example, the computer's name is set to Serpent. By double-clicking on the value of "Computer Name," you can change that name to something else and the value will be changed in the Control Panel.

F I G U R E 6.8

Editing a Registry value

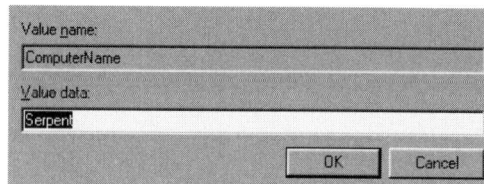

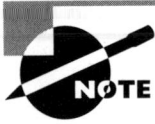

NOTE You don't need to save changes to the Registry. Those changes will be made automatically, without saving them.

STUDY QUESTIONS

Installation Failures

1.   If Setup fails to run at all, what three things should you check for?

_____

_____

_____

2.   True or False: If a user has repeated hangs when running Setup on the hardware-detection phase, they should look at DETCRASH.LOG for information as to what is happening.

3.   Which of the following PCs will not run Windows 95? Why?

A.   286 with 120MB disk and 10MB RAM and a VGA card

B.   486SX with 80MB hard disk, 4MB RAM and an SVGA card

C.   486DX with a 500MB hard disk, 16MB of RAM and an EGA card

_____

_____

_____

4.   Joe is installing Windows 95 from the network, and his connection fails halfway through the installation. What is the first thing that he should do?

_____

5. If the Setup routine fails before reaching the hardware detection stage, what file is used to determine where the Setup failed?

_____

6. What is meant by "Safe detection"?

_____

_____

7. What should you do if Setup fails before running the Hardware Detection phase?

_____

_____

8. What does it mean if you find that Setup failed with a B1 error?

_____

_____

9. Your PC's BIOS has virus-detection capabilities enabled. For best performance, what should you do before running Windows 95 Setup, and why?

_____

_____

10. During installation, you could use the _____
switch with SETUP.EXE if your system hangs when ScanDisk is running.

11. If you're installing from a floppy disk and Setup fails on the second disk, what should you do?

_____

_____

12. What is the most important thing to check for if the Setup process fails when the Windows 95 Startup Wizard is starting to run?

_____

Boot Process Failures

13. True or False: You do not need to have HIMEM.SYS in CONFIG.SYS to run Windows 95.

14. True or False: HIMEM.SYS must be loaded for Windows 95 to run.

15. What is the startup disk?

_____

_____

16. Dave's computer had two internal SCSI hard drives being run off of the same controller. After turning off his computer and removing the second drive, the system no longer boots properly. What is the first thing that Dave should check?

_____

_____

Connectivity Failures

17. Your network is using DHCP for IP address leasing. Which tool can you use to determine your own IP address?

_____

18. True or False: Any user can run the NetWatcher utility on any computer to troubleshoot resource access problems.

19. True or False: You can use a multihomed Windows 95 machine to connect two TCP/IP networks and route traffic between them.

20. Your computer is connected to the Internet with IP address 12.48.92.6 and to the LAN with IP address 192.46.53. If an Internet user sends a message to 192.46.53, will the packet get to you?

_____

21. You're using DHCP to assign addresses for your network. If your network adapter has two IP addresses, how will the DHCP server keep them straight?

_____

_____

_____

22. How can you use Network Neighborhood to disconnect a user from a shared resource on another computer?

_____

_____

Printer Problems

23. True or False: Disabling enhanced metafile spooling may solve some printing problems.

24. Generic/Text Only support is provided with the Windows 95 Universal Printer driver using the _____ file.

25. If your documents look strange after printing, with missing graphics or unformatted text, what is the most likely explanation?

_____

_____

26. Taking steps to resolve printing problems caused by memory shortages will likely make print jobs print more _____.

27. Explain how lack of hard disk space impacts printing.

_____

_____

_____

28. True or False: So long as a print job is text-only with no graphics, you shouldn't run into problems printing if you can print anything at all.

File System Problems

29. How do you disable the use of all 32-bit disk drivers?

_____

_____

30. You create a document in Word 95. You then edit that document in Word 6 running under Windows 95. What will happen to the original file name of the document?

_____

31. True or False: If you disable 32-bit disk drivers, then when you reboot all drives run with those drivers will be available through the use of real-mode drivers.

32. True or False: You will need to disable the use of long file names if you want to run DOS applications.

Resource Access Problems

33. A Windows 95 user on a NetWare network running IPX cannot see other Windows 95 workstations on the other side of a router. What is the first thing that you should check?

_____

34. True or False: Before connecting to a NetWare network, you will need to determine the version of NetWare being run on that network and set frame size accordingly.

35. Where can you set frame size for NetWare networks?

_____

36. To ensure that TCP/IP is working properly, what three systems should you ping?

_____

_____

_____

37. Where would you disable write-behind caching or protected-mode disk access?

_____

38. Your Windows 95 computer running TCP/IP is on Subnet A. What do you need in order to connect to a server on Subnet B?

_____

39. What can you tell about the physical appearance of a network if you know that one of the IP addresses on the network is 145.64.222.5, one is 145.64.222.6, and one is 145.64.219.4?

_____

_____

Device and Device Driver Problems

40. If you bring up Device Manager and see a small yellow symbol with a "!" in it, what does this mean?

_____

41. True or False: A disabled device will not appear in the Device Manager.

Editing the Registry

42. Explain the purpose of the SYSTEM.DA0 and USER.DA0 files.

_____

_____

STUDY QUESTIONS

43. What should you ensure about `<FILENAME>.REG` before double-clicking on it in Explorer?

_____

44. What physical file(s) compose the Registry, and where are they located?

_____

45. When editing the Registry, you're typically editing _____.

6-1 What symbol indicates a resource conflict in the Change Settings dialog box of the System Properties applet?

    A. !

    B. .

    C. *

    D. ?

6-2 A Windows 95 workstation is set up to use the Client for NetWare Networks. When the workstation boots up, there are no errors and no apparent problems with the server, but the user cannot see any of the NetWare servers. What is the most likely cause of the problem?

    A. The network card is not working.

    B. The preferred server is not set properly.

    C. The primary server is down.

    D. The workstation and servers are not using a common protocol.

6-3 When running Setup from MS-DOS, Dave receives the error "Standard Mode: Fault in MS-DOS Extender." The most likely cause of this problem is:

    A. There is insufficient conventional memory.

    B. There is a hardware failure.

    C. There is insufficient extended memory on the computer.

    D. There is a conflict in the upper memory region.

6-4 Kelly is installing Windows 95 from CD-ROM on all of her company's computers. After installing it onto 15 machines without a problem, she gets an error on the 16th machine stating an .INF file cannot be opened. The most probable cause of this problem is:

    A. The .INF file is corrupted.

    B. There is a problem with the CD-ROM.

    C. There is insufficient available memory.

    D. There is a problem with the hard disk drive.

6-5 If a workstation is configured to use TCP/IP properly, how long should it take for the computer to respond to the command `ping 127.0.0.1`?

    A. Immediately

    B. 5 seconds

    C. 10 seconds

    D. 1 minute

6-6 How do you boot to MS-DOS without pressing F8 during system initialization to bring up the Windows 95 boot menu?

    A. Press F4 when the "Starting Windows" message appears.

    B. Press F3 when the "Starting Windows" message appears.

    C. Press the spacebar when the "Starting Windows" message appears.

    D. None of the above.

6-7 If you select an incorrect display driver for your system that cannot be used with your hardware, what will happen?

    A. You must run Setup again and select the correct driver.

    B. You must boot with the emergency boot disk and edit the Registry.

    C. Windows 95 will detect the error and revert to a standard VGA driver.

    D. Windows 95 will boot in Safe Mode so you can change the driver.

6-8 Which of the following will not help if you're having problems with memory overruns? Choose all that apply.

    A. Using EMF for print spooling

    B. Printing TrueType as Graphics

    C. Reducing the number of fonts used in the document

    D. Reducing the numbers of graphical elements in the document

6-9 Your document output is garbled and bears no resemblance to what you're trying to print. Which of the following is the most likely explanation?

    A. Your printer has a shortage of memory.

    B. Your printer server has a shortage of memory.

    C. Too many .EMF files exist in the printer server's TEMP folder.

    D. None of the above.

6-10   Your computer's IP address is 192.76.2.35, and you're on a C-class network. Which of the following cannot be the IP address for the default gateway on your segment? Choose all that apply.

    A. 192.46.2.1

    B. 192.76.2.1

    C. 192.76.2.5

    D. 192.76.5.1

6-11   Choose all that apply. Which of the following are not a possible resolution for the problem of being unable to print at all?

    A. Clear extraneous files from the hard disk.

    B. Check the network connection.

    C. Ping the printer server.

    D. Change the print type to RAW.

6-12   Which of the following tools will permit you to view network shares for a node on a TCP/IP network?

    A. NetWatcher

    B. WinIPCFG

    C. Network Neighborhood

    D. System Monitor

6-13   An incorrectly assigned printer driver will produce:

    A. Missing graphics

    B. Incorrectly formatted or unformatted text

    C. Garbage

    D. No output at all

6-14   Joe is trying to print from his Windows 95 laptop, which has 16MB of memory and a 500MB uncompressed hard drive that's very full. He's not getting any output at all, and examination of the printer job list shows that his jobs are not getting spooled to the printer. Which of the following are likely diagnoses to his problem?

    A. Joe is using the wrong printer driver.

    B. Joe needs more memory installed in his computer.

    C. Joe needs to clear some files from his hard disk.

    D. Joe is not connected properly to the printer.

6-15   If your machine has a static IP address assigned to it, it also needs:

    A. A subnet mask

    B. A DNS server

    C. A WINS server

    D. A DHCP server

6-16   The contents of HKEY_CURRENT_USER apply to:

    A. The user logged in at the moment

    B. The machine settings for the user logged in at the moment

    C. Both machine and user settings for the current user

    D. None of the above

UNIT

7

Final Review

FINAL REVIEW

You've studied the material and taken the unit exams. Now, let's see how you do on a representation of the real thing. The number of questions on each Microsoft certification exam varies, along with the time allotted, but the ratio of time to questions is pretty consistent—you'll have about a minute and a half to two minutes for each question. We've supplied 67 questions here, so give yourself 90–120 minutes to complete the Final Review.

NOTE   Not all the material in the units is covered here in the same level of detail. That's because the exam itself is a bit slanted—much of it seems to cover networking and dial-up networking, printing, and troubleshooting.

All set? Then let's go. Good luck!

1   Your computer's IP address is 201.76.2.35, and you're on a C-class network. Which of the following cannot be the IP address for the default gateway on your segment? Choose all that apply.

    A. 201.46.2.1

    B. 201.76.2.1

    C. 201.76.5.1

    D. 201.76.2.5

2   What command must be included in the MSDOS.SYS file to enable dual-boot in Windows 95?

    A. MultiBoot=1

    B. DoubleBoot=2

    C. BootWin=0

    D. BootMulti=1

3 User profiles are in use on the ORPHEUS domain and enabled on each Windows 95 workstation. Jan, the new temp, does not yet have a user profile. What happens when she logs onto ORPHEUS?

    A. Jan will not be permitted to log on.

    B. A user profile will be created for her, based on the default user profile, and copied to the local computer.

    C. A user profile will be created for her, based on the default user profile, and copied to the network server.

    D. None of the above.

4 What do you need to do to allow you to print from MS-DOS applications to a network printer?

    A. Run the Windows 95 CAPTURE utility.

    B. Run the NET CAPTURE PORT command.

    C. Ensure the LPT port has been captured.

    D. All of the above.

5 You're administering a Windows 95 workgroup running NetBEUI for its transport protocol. At present, the workgroup contains five computers and is working just fine with one master browser, but you'll be adding some more in the near future and are trying to plan for your needs then. According to Microsoft, how many computers must exist in a workgroup before a backup browser is needed?

    A. 10

    B. 30

    C. 20

    D. 15

6   How do you set up a shared network installation of Windows 95?

   A. Run SETUP.EXE /a

   B. Run SETUP.EXE /n

   C. Run INSTALL.EXE

   D. Run NETSETUP.EXE

7   You're setting up a NetWare network with Windows 95 clients. You need to specify a network number for the IPX/SPX protocol to use when:

   A. You would like the workstation to access servers across a router.

   B. You would like the workstation to use SAP.

   C. You would like to install two network cards in the workstation and use Windows 95 internal routing features.

   D. None of the above.

8   Elaine is part of the HR workgroup on the network but wants to see what resources are available in ACCOUNTS. She's working from a DOS application at the moment. What command can she use to view those resources?

   A. NET VIEW /WORKGROUP:ACCOUNTS

   B. NET VIEW

   C. NET VIEW ACCOUNTS

   D. NET VIEW ACCOUNTS/WORKGROUP

9 You suspect a resource conflict between your network card and your sound card. Which tool is recommended to view the settings for each and possibly fix the problem?

A. The Device Manager

B. REGEDIT

C. Running Notepad to view NETWORK.INI and SOUNDCRD.INI

D. The Hardware Profiles tab of the System Properties dialog box

10 You're working in a DOS window. What command can you use to browse the resources shared in your workgroup?

A. NET BROWSE

B. NET SHARE

C. NET VIEW

D. NET USE

11 In the interests of getting better security on your network, you'd like to require that users log into the Windows NT domain before gaining access to Windows 95. What must you do to force users to log into the domain before using Windows 95? Choose all that apply.

A. Use System Policies.

B. Set the Primary Network Logon field.

C. You cannot force a domain login from Windows 95.

D. Add the server to the user profile settings.

12   You need to justify the purchase of MS Plus for Windows 95. Which of the following are features of Compression Agent but are not found in DriveSpace? Choose all that apply.

    A. Compression of drives up to 4GB in size

    B. Compression of individual files and folders within a volume

    C. Taking space from a drive and creating a separate compressed volume

    D. Automatic compression of files that have not been accessed for a predetermined period of time

13   Which of the following is the recommended minimum configuration to host a workgroup fax machine?

    A. 486-based computer with 4MB of RAM running as a dedicated fax server

    B. 386-based computer with 16MB of RAM running as a dedicated fax server

    C. 486-based computer with 12MB of RAM running as a non-dedicated fax server

    D. 386-based computer with 8MB of RAM running as a dedicated fax server

14   What happens if the user profile on the server is newer than the local copy?

    A. The copy on the server is updated.

    B. The local copy is updated.

    C. The two versions are merged.

    D. None of the above.

15   Which protocol must be bound to your dial-up adapter to be able to access the Internet?

    A. NetBEUI

    B. IPX/SPX

    C. TCP/IP

    D. A and C

16   A Windows 95 workstation is set up to use the Client for NetWare Networks. Both the client and the server are using IPX/SPX; the client has been manually configured to use the 802.2 frame type. When the workstation boots up, there are no errors and no apparent problems with the server, but the user cannot see any of the NetWare 3.12 servers. What is the most likely cause of the problem?

    A. The network card is not working.

    B. The preferred server is not set properly.

    C. The frame type is incorrect on the client.

    D. The workstation and servers are not using a common protocol.

17   You're setting up clients for NetWare servers. You have two file servers, one print server, and one communications server. How many NetWare servers can Windows 95 obtain a list of users from for pass-through authentication?

    A. 1

    B. 2

    C. 5

    D. As many as are in the NetWare network

18   Horace logs onto the network and does some work from his desk, changing his color scheme. After lunch, he has a meeting in his supervisor's office and uses his supervisor's computer to log on again to show her some of the work he's been doing on another project. When his supervisor is called away for a moment, Horace changes his screen saver. After the meeting, his supervisor logs him off and logs back in herself, and Horace goes back to his desk to continue working. At the end of the day, Horace logs off his own computer. When Horace logs in in the morning, what changes to his Desktop will he notice?

   A. The user profile will now use the new color scheme and the new screen saver.

   B. Neither the new color scheme nor the new screen saver will be stored in his profile, because the profile was opened twice.

   C. Only the new screen saver is saved.

   D. Only the new color scheme is saved.

19   Where should you store login scripts on Windows NT networks that have both primary and backup domain controllers?

   A. A copy of the login script should be copied to the \Windows\System directory of the PDC.

   B. A copy of the login script should be copied to every domain controller.

   C. A copy of the login script should be copied to the \Windows directory.

   D. None of the above.

20   What is the IP information utility that ships with Windows 95 called?

   A. IPCONFIG

   B. WINIP

   C. WINIPCFG

   D. CFGIP

FINAL REVIEW

21   Ginevra is installing Windows 95 from CD-ROM on all of her company's computers, all of which have different configurations and range from machines for power users to machines that barely make the hardware requirements. After installing it onto 15 machines without a problem, on the 16th machine she gets an error stating that an .INF file cannot be opened. The most probably cause of this problem is:

    A. The .INF file is corrupted.

    B. There is a problem with the CD-ROM.

    C. There is insufficient available memory.

    D. There is insufficient space on the hard disk drive.

22   You're using Windows name resolution on your network and would like to make it as stable as possible. How many WINS servers can be specified?

    A. One—A primary

    B. Two—A primary and a secondary

    C. Three—A primary, secondary, and tertiary

    D. None of the above

23   Windows 95 can automatically download system policies from a NetWare server. Which client must be used for this to occur? Choose all that apply.

    A. VLMs

    B. Microsoft Client for NetWare Networks

    C. NETX

    D. Microsoft Client for Microsoft Networks

24   From the Disk Defragmenter window, what action do you take to override Defrag's default optimization choice?

   A. Click the Choices button.

   B. Click the Options button.

   C. Click the Advanced button.

   D. Click the Change button.

25   Data is stored on disk in logical units called:

   A. Tracks

   B. Clusters

   C. Sectors

   D. Wedges

26   If you select an incorrect display driver for your system that cannot be used with your hardware, what will happen?

   A. You must run Setup again and select the correct driver.

   B. You must boot with the emergency boot disk and edit the Registry.

   C. Windows 95 will detect the error and revert to a standard VGA driver.

   D. Windows 95 will boot in Safe Mode so you can change the driver.

27   Which of the following would be indicated by a high-value Memory: Page Faults? Choose all that apply.

    A. A shortage of physical memory

    B. A need for a faster processor

    C. An application that does not terminate its threads properly

    D. None of the above

28   Your document output is not formatted correctly, and pictures are missing. Which of the following is the most likely explanation?

    A. Your printer has a shortage of memory.

    B. Your print server has a shortage of memory.

    C. Too many .EMF files exist in the printer server's TEMP folder.

    D. You're using the wrong printer driver.

29   You're working on a fast laptop with limited hard disk space. The laptop is the only computer on the network with Microsoft Plus installed. You would like to use the Compression Agent to compress your data. For purposes of compressing data on the office Zip drive that's temporarily attached to the laptop, which compression type would be most useful to you, and why?

    A. UltraPack, compressing all files as they're created and edited

    B. HiPack, compressing all files as they're created and edited

    C. UltraPack, compressing only files older than a certain date

    D. None of the above

30   Which of the following is not a System Monitor category? Choose all that apply. (The wording used here may not be precisely the wording used in the category label.)

> **A.** Client for Microsoft Networks
>
> **B.** Memory Manager
>
> **C.** Evaluation of the Token Ring network
>
> **D.** NetBEUI monitoring

31   Which symbol indicates a resource that isn't working in the Device Manager?

> **A.** !
>
> **B.** .
>
> **C.** *
>
> **D.** ?

32   Given the following output, what is being tested?

Pinging 127.0.0.1 with 32 bytes of data:

Reply from 127.0.0.1: bytes=32 time=1ms TTL=32

Reply from 127.0.0.1: bytes=32 time=1ms TTL=32

Reply from 127.0.0.1: bytes=32 time=1ms TTL=32

Reply from 127.0.0.1: bytes=32 time=1ms TTL=32

> **A.** The connection to the default gateway on a Class-B network
>
> **B.** The connection to the default gateway on a Class-C network
>
> **C.** The connection to a remote host
>
> **D.** The loopback connection

33   Which of the following will not help if you're having problems with slow printing? Choose all that apply.

   A. Using EMF for print spooling

   B. Disabling Print TrueType as Graphics

   C. Reducing the number of fonts used in the document

   D. Reducing the numbers of graphical elements in the document

34   You want to maintain a user account database on a single server and use pass-through authentication. TCP/IP is the protocol of choice. Which of the following are valid choices for a network operating system on the login server?

   A. Windows NT

   B. NetWare

   C. Windows 95

   D. LAN Manager

35   How many UNC connections to network resources does Windows 95 support?

   A. Depends on system memory

   B. 128

   C. 256

   D. Unlimited

36 You have a diverse network and would like to load several network clients onto each Windows 95 client. All clients have lots of memory installed, so RAM limitations are not a serious issue for you. How many network clients can you install in Windows 95?

    A. One real-mode and multiple protected-mode clients

    B. Two real-modes and one protected-mode client

    C. One real-mode and no protected-mode clients

    D. Multiple protected-mode clients and multiple real-mode clients

37 Windows 95 File and Print Services for NetWare supports two mechanisms for advertising shared resources. What are they?

    A. Workgroup Advertising

    B. File Advertising

    C. FPS Advertising

    D. SAP Advertising

38 By default, which users have the right to access computers running the Remote Registry Service from across the network? Choose all that apply.

    A. Administrators

    B. The local user

    C. Power users

    D. All users

39   How much conventional memory does the Client for Microsoft Networks use?

    A. 5KB

    B. 10KB

    C. 50KB

    D. None of the above

40   You're setting up user access in your client/server network. Users log into Windows NT servers, and you're using the domain model rather than the workgroup model. Not all users will log into the same machine at all times. It's important that users employ settings that you specified ahead of time and that those settings follow them from machine to machine. Which of the following choices will fulfill these requirements, if stored on the Primary Domain Controller? Choose all that apply.

    A. Mandatory user profiles

    B. System policies

    C. User profiles

    D. Login scripts

41   You open the System Policy Editor and note that the checkbox next to one option is filled with gray. This means that:

    A. The option is enabled.

    B. The option is disabled.

    C. The option is unavailable.

    D. None of the above.

42 Which of the following actions are required to set up system policies to be loaded from the local machine, rather than from the server? Choose all that apply.

   A. Enable user profiles on the local machine.

   B. Rename CONFIG.POL to USER.POL.

   C. Store the .POL file in the \System folder of your Windows 95 installation.

   D. None of the above.

43 Which of the following protocols would be required to connect to a HP Jet Direct printer connected directly to the network when the login servers are running NetWare? Choose all that apply.

   A. DLC

   B. IPX/SPX-compatible protocol

   C. TCP/IP

   D. PPTP

44 In the System Policy Editor, the password policy settings are as follows:

   • Hide share passwords with asterisks has a blank checkbox next to it.

   • Disable password caching has a gray checkbox next to it.

   • Require alphanumeric Windows password is checked.

   • Minimum Windows password length has a gray checkbox next to it.

You want to make sure that you force Windows 95 users to type in passwords every time, and that their passwords are not visible onscreen when they're being typed in. Which of the following boxes do you need to click on? Choose all that apply.

   A. Hide share passwords with asterisks.

   B. Disable password caching.

   C. Require alphanumeric Windows password.

   D. Minimum Windows password length.

45   A DOS application requires expanded memory. In its Properties dialog box, you need to enable:

   A. DPMI memory

   B. XMS memory

   C. EMS memory

   D. Conventional memory

46   How much expanded memory do you need to install Windows 95 from MS-DOS 6.*x*?

   A. 1MB

   B. 2MB

   C. 3MB

   D. 5MB

47 You're using share-level permissions on your machine, which is part of a Windows NT domain. Joe and Anna are both members of the Users group. How can you make it so that Joe can read and write files on your shared MYFILES directory, but Anna can only read files? Choose all that apply.

A. Assign Full Control permissions to Joe at the Primary Domain Controller.

B. Assign Read Only permissions to Anna at the Primary Domain Controller.

C. Share MYFILES as MYFILES$.

D. Set two passwords on MYFILES: one for Read-Only, and one for Full Control.

48 Which of the following statements about setting up long file name support on a NetWare server are untrue? Choose all that apply.

A. Windows 95 Setup only enables long file names when you're using NetWare 3.12 or later.

B. You must add the line `load os2` to the `STARTUP.NCF` file on the NetWare server.

C. You must copy `OS2.NAM` to the directory on the NetWare server that has `SERVER.EXE` in it.

D. You cannot use both long file names and aliases in a single path statement.

49 Choose all that apply. The `\Mail` directory is used on NetWare servers to store:

A. Mandatory user profiles

B. User profiles

C. System policies

D. None of the above

50   You're connecting to a NetWare 3.12 server and want to use a real-mode client. Which of the following will work? Choose all that apply.

    A. NETX

    B. VLM

    C. Client for NetWare Networks

    D. NWCON

51   Which of the following is a reason to use one of the real-mode NetWare clients supplied by Novell for Windows 95? Choose all that apply.

    A. Faster connection to the server

    B. Support for NDS

    C. Support for bindery services

    D. Support for NetWare IP

52   Your Windows 95 network is using both TCP/IP and IPX/SPX-compatible protocol. The network is logically divided into three workgroups, but those workgroups are physically connected. How many master browsers will there be on the network?

    A. 2

    B. 3

    C. 5

    D. 6

FINAL REVIEW

53 Which of the following services provides host name resolution?

    A. DHCP

    B. DNS

    C. WINS

    D. RFC

54 By default, the host name specified in the DNS settings is:

    A. The local user name

    B. The local computer name

    C. Assigned by the DHCP server

    D. None of the above

55 Which of the following is a fully qualified domain name?

    A. fred@yournetwork.com

    B. fred

    C. yournetwork.com

    D. fred.yournetwork

56 You've got two DNS servers listed in the TCP/IP Properties dialog box so that the second one can take over in case of failure of the first. You attempt to resolve the host name frederica.corp.com, but no entry for this name is found in the primary DNS server. What happens?

    A. The secondary DNS server is queried.

    B. The closest match is supplied.

    C. The DNS server queries the WINS server for name resolution for the NetBIOS name frederica.

    D. The name resolution fails.

57 Which of the following problems might be diagnosed by printing directly to a port?

    A. A spooling problem

    B. An incorrect or corrupt printer driver

    C. An application conflict

    D. None of the above

58 Your NetWare network consists of several NetWare 3.11 servers. One day while you're connected to the network, a new server running NetWare 4.x is added to the network. You cannot connect to the shared resources on this server, or transmit data between your computer and it. Which of the following tactics is most likely to allow you to connect to the new server?

    A. Send a SAP broadcast to the network to restart your browsing connections with all NetWare browsers.

    B. In the IPX/SPX Properties dialog box, change the frame type to 802.2.

    C. Log off the network and log back on again.

    D. You cannot connect to a NetWare environment consisting of more than one NetWare version.

59   A NetWare 4.*x* server has been added to your network. This server uses the network directory services (NDS), not bindery emulation. Which of the following statements are true?

     A. If you install VLM as the Windows 95 client, then you will be able to connect to the server.

     B. You can install NETX to access the server using NDS.

     C. You can use the Client for NetWare Networks if you change the frame type from Auto to 802.2.

     D. With the right client installed, you can store user profiles on this server.

60   In which situation would you would install NetBIOS over IPX/SPX?

     A. To reduce data transmission time on NetWare networks, as NetBIOS is a faster protocol than is IPX/SPX

     B. To make NetBEUI traffic routable

     C. To permit network applications that require access to the NetBIOS commands to run on a NetWare network

     D. To take over in case of protocol or transmission errors in the main transport protocol, if IPX/SPX-compatible

61   You're choosing a data protocol to use for Dial-up Networking to a Windows NT 4.0 server. Which of the following might you choose?

     A. PPP

     B. TCP/IP

     C. DLC

     D. NetBEUI

62   Which of the following line protocols can you use to connect to the Internet?

    A. SLIP

    B. TCP/IP

    C. PPP

    D. NetBEUI

63   Which of the following are reasons to make network connections with UNC names rather than by mapping drive letters to resources? Choose all that apply.

    A. When you access a UNC path not available on the local network, Windows 95 will not reject the connection but will attempt to connect with Dial-up Networking.

    B. Mapping drive letters only lets you connect to up to 26 network resources.

    C. Connecting to UNC resources consumes less memory than does mapping resources to drive letters.

    D. If a UNC resource moves, Windows 95 will browse for the resource.

64   When accessing a NetWare server across a dial-up connection, which Windows 95 line protocol should you use?

    A. TCP/IP

    B. PPP

    C. IPX/SPX

    D. None of the above

65   You're creating a dial-up connection to a Windows NT 3.1 Advanced Server machine. Which of the following line protocol types should you choose to make the connection?

   A. PPP.

   B. SLIP.

   C. RAS.

   D. Windows NT 3.1 does not support dial-up services.

66   Your computer is currently a node on a Windows 95 network, and you're setting up a dial-up connection to a Windows NT 4.0 computer for it. Which of the following must you do to set up the connection? Choose all that apply.

   A. Install the Client for Microsoft Networks

   B. Specify PPP as the line protocol

   C. Choose a data protocol for the connection

   D. None of the above

67   Under what circumstances would you need to specify an IP address for an Internet connection? Choose all that apply.

   A. Always

   B. When no DNS server is in use at the ISP

   C. When no WINS server is in use at the ISP

   D. When no DHCP server is in use at the ISP

APPENDIX

Study Question and
Sample Test Answers

Unit 1 Answers

Study Questions

Choosing a Workgroup or Domain

1. Windows NT

   Explanation: Windows NT supports the NTFS file system, which permits file-level security at the local level. FAT and its variations, used by Windows 95, does not offer file-level security.

2. False

   Explanation: Windows 95 does not support NTFS.

3. There aren't any differences.

4. A and B

   Explanation: Only the 32-bit clients will provide support for long file names. The clients written to work with a 16-bit operating system have no need for such support.

5. Windows NT (Server or Workstation)
   LAN Manager
   Windows for Workgroups

6. False

   Explanation: You'll need a computer that can store an accounts database, but membership in a domain is not required—this Windows NT computer could be part of a workgroup.

7. Security accounts database

8. All network access is managed through the Primary Domain Controller, rather than for each node in the network. You can set permissions for all resources and define all access from a single point.

9. False

    Explanation: A Windows NT network is only a domain if one Windows NT Server machine has been made the Primary Domain Controller. If it's just a server, then the network is organized as a workgroup.

10. Probably more, because each user would have to manage access to the resources made available from his or her computer.

Developing a Security Strategy

11. Remote administration must be enabled.
    User-level security must be enabled.
    The remote Registry service must be installed.

    Explanation: You can use remote Registry editing to configure client machines across the network. It's a powerful tool, so be sure to only provide support for this when needed.

12. In the SYS:PUBLIC folder on the preferred server

13. In the netlogon share on the Primary Domain Controller (PDC)

14. A custom Program folder
    A custom Network Neighborhood
    A custom Desktop icons
    A custom Start menu
    A custom startup folder

    Explanation: Any settings not defined in these folders will result in the default options being used.

15. Remote administration is enabled for the Domain Administrators group on NT networks and for the Supervisor or Admin user on NetWare networks.

    Explanation: These groups are roughly equivalent on Windows NT and NetWare networks, giving members of those groups near-universal powers.

16. False

    Explanation: Remote administration requires enabling of the Remote Registry Service, enabling of user-level security, and enabling of Remote Administration.

17. USER.MAN

    Explanation: When USER.MAN is specified, it overwrites USER.DAT to create the user settings.

18. System policies can be applied selectively, whereas mandatory user profiles control all user-specific settings.
    Mandatory user profiles also do not let you assign computer specific settings.

    Explanation: You can only create one mandatory profile, but you can create a number of profiles that users cannot change. If you need more than one user profile but don't want it changed, consider making the profiles read-only.

19. System policies

    Explanation: System policies are loaded during logon and overwrite any previously existing settings, whereas user profiles replace USER.DAT.

20. The Desktop folder
    The Recent folder
    The Start menu folder
    The Program folder
    USER.DAT
    USER.DA0

    Explanation: The SYSTEM.DAT and .DA0 files are not part of a user profile because they are computer-specific.

21. The policy "Remove 'Run' command" with the Restrictions subgroup of Shell

    Explanation: This policy is user and group-specific.

22. True

    Explanation: You will have to do some extra work to arrange manual downloading of system policies, as real-mode clients cannot read long file names.

23. `ADMIN.ADM` located in the `System` folder

    Explanation: The default template is a set of standard system policies that you can use to create your custom user policies. You can create your own templates as well.

24. False

    Explanation: The profile will only reflect settings in use on the last PC the user logs off from, assuming the user is allowed to change his or her policy.

25. False

    Explanation: To specify all user settings, mandatory user profiles must be used.

26. Control Panel
    Desktop
    Network
    Shell
    System

27. True

    Explanation: System policies may be created for either users or machines. Groups are a superset of users.

28. False

    Explanation: When your computer is using share-level security, you can only connect to other computers using share-level security.

29. System policies
    User profiles

30. False

    Explanation: By default, user profiles include both Desktop settings and network connections.

31. The most recent one, based on timestamp

32. Passwords

33. False

    Explanation: User settings can include a workgroup name.

34. Mandatory user profiles assign settings that must be applied to all workstations to which they're assigned, whereas system policies allow you to choose parts of the user environment to control and some to leave to the users' discretion.

35. User

Sample Test

1-1   C

   Explanation: The default user profile will be loaded into the system Registry, into the HKEY_CURRENT_USER key.

1-2   A

   Explanation: This tab will not appear until the Remote Administration feature is enabled.

1-3   B

   Explanation: System policies are assigned to users (or machines). As users are defined by their names and group memberships, policies are assigned to those names and group memberships.

1-4   D

1-5   A

1-6   A

1-7   B

Explanation: This option contains settings you can use to prevent the user from accessing any or all tabs of the Passwords applet.

1-8   A

Explanation: File and Printer Sharing for NetWare networks controls SAP advertising, Control Panel controls access to Control Panel applets, and Sharing settings determine whether you can override resource sharing restrictions.

1-9   C

1-10   C

Unit 2 Answers

Study Questions

Installing Windows 95

1. False

2. NETSETUP.EXE

   Explanation: NETSETUP.EXE is used to create a flat copy of Windows 95 on a server so that Setup may be run from that server. The utility is found on the Windows 95 CD-ROM.

3. BootMulti=1

   Explanation: MSDOS.SYS is both a read-only and a hidden file, so you'll have to use Find (or instruct Explorer to show hidden files) and remove the read-only attribute before you can add the BootMulti=1 setting, which is not in the file by default.

4. PROTOCOL.INI, SYSTEM.INI, and WIN.INI

   Explanation. These three .INI files form the core of the Windows information migrated during the upgrade.

5. Run GRPCONV.EXE /m.

   Explanation: GRPCONV.EXE runs automatically during Setup, but you can also run it manually.

6. Install Windows 95 into/over your existing Windows directory.

   Explanation: Although it's a good idea to back up before installing any new operating system, Windows 95 is designed to smoothly upgrade your Windows 3.x installation and maintain all applicable settings.

7. True

8. False

   Explanation: Windows 95 will keep or migrate all existing settings and files to continue to run your applications. The only applications that might present a problem are those incompatible with Windows 95, for which you may need to edit your system configuration or run a compatibility utility.

9. Typical, Portable, Compact, and Custom

   Explanation: Each of the installation options is presented for a particular situation so that, for example, someone installing Windows 95 onto a laptop can automatically install the options most likely needed instead of choosing from the options offered by Custom.

10. MSBATCH.INF

   Explanation: MSBATCH.INF is a Setup script that defines how Windows 95 is installed.

11. WRKGRP.INI

   Explanation: WRKGRP.INI should be stored in the shared directory that contains the Windows 95 source files.

12. True

Explanation: However, you need OS/2 set up to dual-boot (using OS/2's Boot Manager) to DOS before you install and you need to replace the OS/2 loader after Windows 95 installation (or you can install just Boot Manager, then install DOS first, then OS/2).

13. True

Explanation: When both Windows NT and Windows 95 are installed on the same computer, the Windows NT boot loader will display a menu of the available operating systems. Windows NT is the default unless specified otherwise in BOOT.INI.

14. 420KB

15. Desktop Computer, Mobile or Docking System, and Network Server

Explanation: The three different roles allocate different amounts of memory to the task of caching files and folders for quicker retrieval. The more files and folders the system can "remember," the more memory is required for the task, so a computer set up as a network server will use more memory than one set up to be a mobile workstation.

16. True

Explanation: However, some of the missing files are available from online sources such as Microsoft's Web site.

17. No (or very little) hard disk space is needed at the local computer, updating drivers and other Windows 95 components is easier, and the Windows 95 installation is protected by network security.

Explanation: Although running Windows 95 over the network may impact system performance, it has some advantages for computers with little disk space, and it makes administration easier.

18. Floppy, RPL Boot PROM

Explanation: Not all Windows systems have hard disks and boot locally. Those booted from the network have a special piece of firmware called a boot PROM (programmable read-only memory).

19. NETLOG.TXT

    Explanation: NETLOG.TXT is created during the network installation portion of Setup and describes each step of the installation and initialization process.

20. These are configuration files.

    Explanation: Dual-boot works by renaming IO, MSDOS, COMMAND, CONFIG, and AUTOEXEC with the .W40 and .DOS extensions. Whichever operating system is booted, the other OS's configuration files will be assigned new extensions accordingly.

21. MSBATCH.INF

    Explanation: The MSBATCH.INF file is a script that may be used for server-based Setup, either to install Windows 95 on individual computers or to create other versions of the Setup script. It records the Setup options specified for an installation.

22. False

    Explanation: Although you can install Windows 95 over DOS 3.31 or later, you cannot set up the system for dual-boot with DOS if you're running a version of DOS prior to 5.0, or running any version of DR-DOS.

23. Yes. 5.0 and 6.x.

    Explanation: Although you can install Windows 95 over versions of DOS 3.31 and later, only versions 5.0 and 6.x are compatible with dual-booting.

24. False

    Explanation: This is true only if the computer boots from the hard disk. Windows 95 introduces the idea of "machine directories" that allow for storing the hardware configuration for a computer. NETSETUP can replicate these directories.

25. False

    Explanation: According to Microsoft, a Windows 95 upgrade from Windows 3.x should take about 35–45MB of hard disk space.

26. True

     Explanation: If there is enough free space *and* if you can boot to DOS/Win3.*x* to run
     Setup. You cannot run Windows 95 Setup from within Windows NT.

27. True

     Explanation: The versions of FAT used by Windows NT and Windows 95 are fully com-
     patible across both operating systems.

28. No option

     Explanation: You cannot edit the MSBATCH.INF file when using server-based Setup. To edit
     MSBATCH.INF, you'll need to use a text editor such as Notepad.

29. Portable

     Explanation: The Portable installation option is designed for use with laptop computers,
     so it's assumed that its users will need a tool like the Briefcase to move files from one com-
     puter to another.

30. \windows\start menu\programs

     Explanation: The .GRP files contain the configuration information for program groups and
     shortcuts.

31. /id

     Explanation: If you use this switch and there isn't enough disk space, you'll have to abort
     Setup anyway.

32. /iq

     Explanation: ScanDisk checks for disk errors, so it's not necessarily a good idea to disable
     this part of Setup.

33. Compact

     Explanation: The Compact installation only requires about 30MB of disk space, when
     installed on a blank hard disk.

34. Custom

Explanation: The Custom installation option requires the most user input of all installation options but also provides the most control over what components are installed.

35. False

Explanation: The disk must be formatted before running Setup.

36. Superior performance, less network traffic, and workstations continue to run when the server is down.

Explanation: If you have the disk space available, you'll get better performance running Windows 95 (or any application) locally, instead of making it vulnerable to delays caused by network traffic.

37. 4

Explanation: If you install a new network adapter, it is automatically bound to all NDIS protocols on the computer.

38. Setup's detection and actions for NetWare TSRs and components.

Explanation: The information recorded by NETDET.INI is used to add custom entries for detecting components of NetWare networks, but is not necessary in all cases.

39. False

Explanation: A FAT partition must exist on the computer before you can install Windows 95. Windows 95's Setup program requires FAT to run. It cannot recognize an HPFS partition.

40. MACHINES.INI

Explanation: MACHINES.INI will contain a separate section for each remote-boot workstation or floppy-booting computer.

41. Running Windows 95 from a server login script with Setup scripts to create a mandatory automated installation.

Explanation: Push installations are used to install Windows 95 remotely, without going to each computer to perform the installation.

42. Create an entry in STARTUP.GRP to run Setup with a script file.

Explanation: When the user starts up Windows, the entry in the Startup folder will automatically begin the upgrade.

43. True

Explanation: The Windows 95 source files installed on the server are the basis of the shared installation, so the server must be a Windows 95 computer.

44. 90

Explanation: The 90MB is required to hold the Windows 95 source files.

45. AUTOEXEC.DOS

Explanation: AUTOEXEC.DOS's purpose is to preserve the pre-installation settings in case you should choose to uninstall Windows 95.

46. New

47. OS/2
NT

48. /is; it will run SETUP.EXE without performing the ScanDisk quick check.

49. False

Explanation: You must be running DOS 5 or later.

Installing and Configuring Network Components

50. Bindings

    Explanation: Bindings information tells which protocols are set up to be used with (bound to) which services and adapters. If more than one protocol is bound to an adapter, the binding order will determine which protocol is used first.

51. IPX/SPX-compatible, TCP/IP, and NetBEUI

    Explanation: You can load more than one of these protocols at once, but it will impact your system resources.

52. From the Network Properties dialog box select Add ➤ Adapter ➤ Intel and then pick the correct Intel adapter.

    Explanation: The adapter may be further configured if necessary by clicking on the Properties button while the adapter is highlighted in the list of installed network components.

53. There can be only one Browse Master for each protocol in use.

54. As many as you need

    Explanation: Windows 95 supports a large number of protected-mode network clients. Protected-mode network clients do not interfere with each other as real-mode clients do; that is, they can interfere with each other, but under normal circumstances do not.

55. Higher version

    Explanation: There is a hierarchy among Microsoft NOSes of who becomes a backup or master browser before the others. Unless a computer has been specifically prevented from becoming a backup or master browser, this hierarchy will be followed.

56. True

    Explanation: True for the most part—in some cases, the older drivers have been replaced by others of the same name which are NDIS 3.1–compatible.

57. False

    Explanation: You cannot mix real-mode and protected-mode networking components on a shared installation.

58. False

    Explanation: There is no real-mode TCP/IP protocol to load Windows 95 with. You need to use IPX/SPX or NetBEUI.

59. Nothing. Detection is automatic by Windows 95.

    Explanation: When you turn on the machine after installing a new PnP device, you'll see a message informing you that new hardware has been detected and the driver is being loaded.

60. You need both NDIS2 and NDIS3.1 drivers, the NDIS2 to start the network in real mode and the NDIS3.1 drivers to take over from the NDIS2 ones in protected mode.

61. NDIS 2 drivers support a transition to protected-mode networking as Windows loads.

    Explanation: Any other real-mode network driver can be used to run Windows 95 without protected-mode networking support.

62. From Control Panel, select the Network applet. Select a transport protocol and click on the Properties button.

    Explanation: Different transport protocols have different properties, so your options will depend on which protocol you're adjusting.

63. 10

    Explanation: This setting is configured in the NetBEUI Properties dialog box.

64. False

    Explanation: One of the subnets will use the default subnet mask; others will use different subnet masks to identify themselves.

65. True

66. Each subnet has a subnet mask. For an IP address in to be on a specific subnet, it must have 1s in all the same locations as does the mask, up to the point at which the mask ends (reading the address and mask in binary form).

67. False

    Explanation: The domain name requested (not required) by DNS refers to Internet domains, not Windows NT domains.

68. By when the server is added

69. Static
    Dynamic

70. False

    Explanation: A Scope ID identifies the collection of computers that all recognize a particular NetBIOS name-IP address mapping.

71. Both DNS servers and gateways are searched in the order in which they're added, but whereas a second DNS server is only searched if the first is not functioning, a second gateway will be searched if the first can't supply a path to the next subnet.

72. IPX/SPX-compatible protocol

73. You don't need to. The default is Auto, and as Windows 95 machines have lower precedence in browser elections than do Windows NT machines, the Windows NT machines will always beat it in an election.

Installing and Configuring Hardware

74. Enhanced Metafile

    Explanation: EMF spooling returns control to the printer more quickly than does spooling RAW data so that print jobs take less work time away from the user.

75. True

Explanation: Some PnP BIOSes do not meet the PnP BIOS version 1.0a requirements; computers with such BIOSes will not be recognized as PnP systems until upgraded to version 1.0a.

76. Add New Hardware

Explanation: Not all hardware will require the Add New Hardware applet; PC-Card adapters, for example, will be automatically detected.

77. True

Explanation: Doing so may impair Windows 95's ability to dynamically allocate resources.

78. Use the Add New Hardware Wizard from Control Panel.

Explanation: The only time this is unnecessary is when PnP is fully supported by the new hardware, as in a PC-Card device. In that case, Windows 95 will detect and configure the new hardware.

79. Double-click on the device in Device Manager, click Driver, and click Change to access the Select Device dialog box.

Explanation: Periodically, device manufacturers release new versions of their drivers. You can use this procedure to upgrade to the new driver.

80. Either ensure that the card's jumper settings have been changed to match, or run the card's software configuration program.

Explanation: Which you do depends on whether the card is configured with hardware or software.

81. False

Explanation: ISA and EISA are two different bus architectures used for adapter cards. ISA is the more common of the two, particularly as EISA's more powerful architecture has been replaced by PCI.

82. You don't. TAPI allows applications to use modems installed centrally in Windows 95.

    Explanation: TAPI-aware applications don't need to provide their own support for modems, but can plug into the telephony interface.

83. Once

    Explanation: All communications applications will read the information stored in TELEPHON.INI to learn how to dial out.

84. True

    Explanation: If you like, you can choose to manually specify a modem, but if the wizard can't find it, chances are the modem is not properly connected or there is a resource conflict.

Installing and Configuring Backup Hardware and Software

85. Full
    Incremental

86. False

    Explanation: Backup supports backing up to any connected directory, even one on the local hard disk.

87. Create a backup set by saving the settings when you have the files/folders to be backed up selected and a destination directory specified.

Sample Test

2-1   C

    Explanation: An .INF file is a text file divided into several parts, each defining information needed for Windows 95 to load the device's drivers and set it up properly.

2-2   D

Explanation: Like the master browser, the backup browse servers maintain lists of network resources, which they get by periodically querying the master browser. Having backup browsers reduces some of the strain on the master browser.

2-3   D

2-4   B

Explanation: The /RPL parameter specifies that Setup should create a disk image on the server for a remote-boot workstation to use during workstation Setup. For this option to work, the Workstation Setup value must also be enabled.

2-5   A

Explanation: Setup is a 16-bit application because the 32-bit operating system hasn't yet been installed, but runs in the protected-mode Windows environment.

2-6   B and C

Explanation: The machine directory contains all settings for a specific machine, including the .INI files and printer spool file, although not mentioned in the question.

2-7   D

Explanation: You must run NETSETUP.EXE (found in the \admin\nettools\netsetup directory on the Windows 95 CD ROM) from an existing local copy of Windows 95. When running NETSETUP, you'll be prompted for the network path of the copy of Windows 95. From that point, you must run Setup.

2-8   D

Explanation: Microsoft wrote the NetWare client to automatically detect the network frame type and network number, so as to save time for network administrators.

2-9   A

Explanation: Only one real-mode network client can run at a time as they're not aware of other clients and would not cooperate with each other.

2-10 A

Explanation: The Modem Installation Wizard is only required for internal or external modems. PC-Card modems will be installed automatically when inserted.

2-11 A

Explanation: The Device Manager controls device settings; although it exchanges information with the Registry, editing the Registry is more prone to dangerous mistakes than is using the GUI interface. POLEDIT and profiles have nothing to do with device settings.

2-12 B

Explanation: ISA configuration information is stored statically because it only changes when you change it. Unless you edit its configuration options, it will continue using the same resources.

2-13 A and D

Explanation: These mappers are necessary to convert the real-mode NDIS 2 drivers to protected-mode drivers that will work with Windows 95.

2-14 B

2-15 C

Explanation: A DNS (Domain Name Service) server maps IP addresses to fully qualified domain names.

2-16 A

2-17 D

Explanation: According to Microsoft, you should use a backup browser when the number of nodes in the network exceeds 15, to reduce the strain on the master browser listing all network resources.

2-18 D

> **Explanation:** Bindings refer to the order in which transport protocols are used by a network adapter to send data across the network. Being at the top of a network adapter's bindings means that that protocol will be used first, and successive protocols only if a connection cannot be reached with the first one.

Unit 3 Answers

Study Questions

Setting Access Permissions for Shared Folders

1. Read-Only, Full, and Depends on Password

2. Pass-through authentication

3. Windows 95 uses the accounts database of an NT Domain or NetWare server to validate access to local resources by other clients. Pass-through authentication refers to the fact that the accounts database resides on another computer than the one being connected to.

4. User-level

5. False

   Explanation: Users can still start Windows 95 in safe mode or from a floppy disk. Windows NT is the only secure Microsoft operating system, as it does not provide these back doors to the operating system.

6. False

   Explanation: Only NetWare and Windows NT servers can provide pass-through authentication.

7. File and print services

8. The local password list file (.PWL) associated with that user

9. In the Access Control tab of the Network properties dialog box

10. User level
    Share level

11. Microsoft NT Servers acting as domain controllers
    NetWare Servers that support the NetWare Bindery

    Explanation: Both Windows NT and the Bindery are dependent on a user object to determine user rights and permissions, so they require a login to their centralized database.

12. False

    Explanation: You can only set passwords on shares if you're using share-level security, not user-level security.

13. Pass-through security

    Explanation: Windows 95 does not maintain its own security accounts database, so it must rely on servers that do.

Creating, Sharing, and Monitoring Network Resources

14. 15
    45

15. There should not be a colon (:) after SYS.

16. Type the server name in the Run dialog box available from the Start menu (e.g. \\myserver).

17. False

    Explanation: Windows 95 users in the same workgroup can share the same fax modem. The Exchange mailbox on the fax server collects all faxes and routes them to the intended recipient.

18. True

19. True

20. Yes, by selecting View ➤ Options and then moving to the File Types tab

21. False

    Explanation: MS Fax is integrated with the Exchange client and can only receive faxes in cooperation with the Exchange client.

22. All machines in your workgroup and/or domain

23. False

    Explanation: .LNK extensions are hidden regardless of this setting.

24. Select the required resource from Network Neighborhood, right-click on it, and select Map Network Drive from the pop-up menu that appears. You can also map a network drive from Windows Explorer, selecting the Map Drive option and choosing the shared drive or folder to connect to.

25. True

26. False

    Explanation: Although the maximum LFN size is 255 characters, the full path name can only be 260 characters.

27. From the Sharing tab in the printer Properties dialog box

28. True

Explanation: `NET VIEW` will provide a list of available resources in the specified server or workgroup (it will not provide a list of available workgroups) and will show NetWare print queues if you are logged onto the NetWare print server.

29. `\\myserver\sys\public`

30. True

Explanation: As a shortcut is only an alias to the more complex path, this will work for both local and network-accessible resources. The only time that these shortcuts won't work is when the network is not running.

31. Right-click on the drive icon and select Sharing.
Highlight the drive icon and select File from the main menu and then Sharing.

32. Select View and then Refresh.

33. True

Explanation: Background print rendering reduces the time it takes to restore control of the application to the user, but creating a print image in the background does take memory and thus could impact low-memory systems.

34. `MSPSRV.EXE` is the Microsoft Print Services for NetWare utility that allows your computer to run as a print server for a NetWare file server.

35. Within the Properties window of the printer, select the Details tab and then the Spool Settings option. From the window provided, you can then alter the Spool Data format option.

36. From the Network applet in the Control Panel, click Add.
Within the Select Network Component Type dialog box, select Service and then click Add. Within the Select Network Service dialog box, click Have Disk and then enter the path `ADMIN\NETTOOLS\PRTAGENT`.

37. `\\nw410-1\sys\public\nwadmin.exe`

38. In the Microsoft Fax properties dialog box, you must select the Let Other People on the Network Use My Modem option on the Modem tab.

39. Network Neighborhood

40. Quick Logon

Explanation: With Quick Logon (as With Ghosted Connections), Windows 95 maps drive letters to persistent connections but does not actually make the connection until the user tries to access it. This speeds up the logon process, and is the default option.

41. D
A
C
B

42. \\orion\"working copy"

43. Yes, it will work, but only one client at a time will be able to dial into the server.

44. Exchange

Explanation: Faxes come into the fax server and are stored in the Exchange mailbox for routing to the intended recipients.

45. Full Access

Setting Up System Policies and User Profiles

46. HKEY_USERs

Explanation: HKEY USERs stores profile information for all users who have logged on already, as well as a default profile for those with no set profile. Each user has their own subkey in this key.

47. CONFIG.POL
SYS:\PUBLIC

48. Options

49. Programs/Accessories/System Tools

50. Select the Passwords applet.
Select the User Profiles tab.
Select the option allowing users to customize their preferences and desktop settings.

51. Registry
Policy File

52. Load balancing

Explanation: On Windows NT networks, the login server is not necessarily the primary domain controller, but may be a backup domain controller, so as to reduce strain on the PDC's resources. To make load balancing work, you'll need to keep a copy of the user profile on all backup domain controllers.

53. True

54. CONFIG.POL is the file, and it implements system policies.

55. You can't.

Explanation: If you must assign policies to a group, the group must already exist on the NetWare or NT network. System Policy Editor has no group-creating capabilities.

56. Both in the \Profiles directory in the local Windows directory and in the user's Home Directory on a server, if applicable.

57. False

Explanation: USER.DAT supplies the information found in HKEY_CURRENT_USER, which are all the settings for the person presently logged in.

58. True

Backing Up and Restoring Data

59. False

Explanation: Microsoft Backup supports the QIC 113 backup tape specification, while MS-DOS's backup utilities use a different one.

60. /p

Explanation: LFNBK is a Windows 95 utility with which you can back up long file names so that they won't be destroyed by legacy disk utilities.

61. Windows 95's Backup utility does not support differential backups. (Yes, this is a trick question.)

Explanation: Differential backups, supported by Windows NT Backup but not Windows 95, are designed to look for files changed or added since the last full backup.

62. False

Explanation: Microsoft Backup supports QIC 113, which in turn, supports long file names.

Managing Hard Disks

63. FDISK

64. False

65. You should use the partition utility that was initially used to create the drive. (Do *not* use FDISK.)

Explanation: SpeedStor and like partitioning utilities replace the BIOS for MS-DOS–disk controller interactions. FDISK will not be able to work with the partition.

66. Compressed Volume File (CVF)

67. True

68. Adjust Free Space

69. False

Explanation: Not only can you adjust the compression ration, but different kinds of files compress at different rates.

70. False

Explanation: Compressed volumes are only locally readable from Windows 95, but they may be read across the network by machines running other operating systems.

71. DriveSpace requires a certain amount of free space to compress a volume. You must run the compression algorithm before the disk is full.

72. Repartitioning a drive deletes all the data on it, and that data is in use when the system is running. To repartition a boot drive, you must boot from a floppy disk.

73. Active

Setting Up Application Environments

74. APPS.INF

Explanation: The APPS.INF file contains a list of master settings for MS-DOS applications. When you run an application listed in APPS.INF, Windows 95 creates a PIF for that application.

75. EMS (or Expanded)
Page

Explanation: The expanded memory page frame is an area in the Upper Memory Area of the MS-DOS memory layout. Expanded memory is divided into 16KB pages.

76. False

77. 60

Explanation: This setting, included for compatibility with older MS-DOS applications, specifies the number of file handle buffers to create. It is not required by Windows 95.

78. False

Explanation: MS-DOS Protected Mode Memory (DPMI) provides an interface to allow applications to switch the 286 processor to protected mode and thus allocate extended memory. Windows applications already execute in protected mode and thus don't need DPMI memory.

79. Right-click and select Properties from the pop-up menu.

80. NOEMS

81. False

82. [PIF95]

83. They are all shut down, including protected-mode network clients.

Sample Test

3-1   C

Explanation: Enhanced Metafile Spooling uses system memory to create an image of the print job to be sent to the printer, running in the background.

3-2   B

3-3   A and D

3-4   D

Explanation: UNC connections are not limited in number like mapped connections because they're not dependent on having an available drive letter—additional mapped connections can only be made so long as drive letters are available.

3-5   C

3-6   C

Explanation: Typing NET VIEW on its own shows a list of available resources in your workgroup, while including the name of a specific server shows the resources on that server.

3-7   A

3-8   A

Explanation: This command will retrieve the browse list stored by the master browser. If you can browse the workgroup with this command but could not otherwise, it may indicate that the backup browser hasn't been updated recently.

3-9   C

3-10 B

3-11 D

3-12 D

3-13 A and C

3-14 A and C

3-15 A

3-16 C

Explanation: The default Windows 95 security is share-level, which means that you cannot restrict printer access based on User or Group ID.

3-17 B

3-18 A

3-19 A and D

Explanation: DOS machines don't handle share names of more than eight letters or handle them well if there's a space in the name (NET SHARE would technically work, but it would have to be enclosed in quotes whenever you referred to it).

3-20 C

3-21 B

Unit 4 Answers

Study Questions

Windows 95 and Windows NT

1. Primary Network Logon

2. `VREDIR.VXD`

3. True

   Explanation: The first time a user logs into Windows 95, separate logins are required for all networks, and another for Windows 95. If all passwords are set to be the same, however, then a single logon may be used.

4. File and Print Services for Microsoft Networks
   File and Print services for NetWare Networks

   Explanation: Other server services are provided by their network manufacturers, but these are the two developed by Microsoft.

5. MS Net login scripts (NT Server and LAN Manager) and NetWare login scripts

6. False

   Explanation: If logon validation is enabled, Windows 95 will attempt to validate the login in an Windows NT domain controller by default.

Windows 95 and NetWare

7. A preferred server must be specified.

8. False

   Explanation. Client for NetWare Networks is the first protected-mode network client for NetWare networks. Prior to its development, network clients were real-mode, and developed by Novell.

9. VLMs

10. False

    Explanation: A NetWare file server is needed for pass-through authentication.

11. False

12. File and Print Services for NetWare must be installed.
    A NetWare server must be specified for pass-through authentication.
    SAP advertising must be enabled.

    Explanation: NetWare server must be identified to hold the accounts database, as the bindery uses user login objects to determine who has access to what objects. SAP advertising is used by NetWare networks to browse available resources, File and Print Services makes resources available on the NetWare network.

13. True

    Explanation: So long as the user name and password are the same for the NetWare logon as for the Windows 95 logon, after the first attempt the logon to the NetWare server will be automatic.

14. The login directory is not mapped to the first network drive by Microsoft's login script processor.

15. False

    Explanation: As the program runs in protected mode, real-mode TSRs cannot be used.

16. None

17. False

    Explanation: LOGIN.EXE should never be used with MS Client for NetWare, but only with Novell's real-mode clients.

18. False

    Explanation: You can only have one NetWare client installed at a time.

19. None

    Explanation: Client for Microsoft Networks is a protected-mode client, and as such uses no conventional memory.

20. DOS Requester (VLMs)

    Explanation: The Client for NetWare Networks does not support NCP Packet Signatures.

21. It's limited to the number of available drive letters for mappings.

22. False

    Explanation: The client supports neither. You must use IPX/SPX-compatible protocol to connect to NetWare servers.

23. 2.x, 3.x and 4.x (4.x under Bindery Emulation)

    Explanation: The NFS file system available with (and native to) NetWare 4.x is not supported; it must emulate an earlier version.

24. False

    Explanation: Using the Client for NetWare Networks, you can only access NetWare 4.1 servers under bindery emulation.

25. Polling
    15

    Explanation: The polling rate determines how often the system checks for waiting print jobs. Polling takes resources, so frequent polling will impact system resources. Infrequent polling will slow print jobs, however.

26. The ID used for Windows and NetWare must be the same and both must use the same password.

    Explanation: If these are the same, the user will still be prompted to enter his name and password twice the first time he logs on, but not after that.

27. She will not be able to download additional folders (such as the Start menu) from the server.

    Explanation: To add long file name support, configure the NetWare volumes with the OS/2 namespace to make them follow HPFS naming conventions.

28. Client for NetWare Networks (protected mode)
    NETX (real mode)
    VLM (real mode)

29. You'll use the VLM client and the 802.2 frame type.

30. VLM

31. False

    Explanation: Although the Client for NetWare Networks does not support IP, both NETX and VLM do.

32. False

    Explanation: Although the Client for NetWare networks supports user profiles and the real-mode NetWare clients support IP, you can't run two clients at the same time.

33. RIP

Windows 95 and the Internet

34. No, they are stored in the TELEPHON.INI file.

    Explanation: They are maintained in the file TELEPHON.INI to provide backward compatibility for 16-bit communications applications.

35. The ID you used when logged on to Windows.

36. True

   Explanation: You'd potentially need to manually enter information if you need to manually log onto your ISP's server with a password, or to specify another default gateway.

37. To allow you to enter any special AT modem commands that would be required to establish the connection.

   Explanation: A terminal window may be used to meet special security requirements held by some servers, or to specify a new default gateway.

38. A comma (,) will pause dialing for two seconds and a ? will display an on-screen prompt to continue dialing.

39. Gateway

   Explanation: The dynamic host configuration protocol (DHCP) server runs from a Windows NT machine, allowing the network administrator to specify a range of IP addresses that may be automatically assigned to computers on the network.

40. On the DNS Configuration tab

41. She can't. SLIP support is only available if Windows 95 was purchased on CD-ROM (although it can be downloaded).

42. `ping ftp.microsoft.com`

   Explanation: Successfully pinging the name rather than the IP address means that name resolution is working.

43. Ping

Windows 95 and Dial-up Networking for Remote Access

44. False

Explanation: Windows 95 supports implicit connections for servers accessed with UNC. If it can't find the resource on the local network, it will prompt you to establish a dial-up connection.

45. False

Explanation: You must use this line protocol if you're dialing directly into a NetWare server, but you can dial into a Microsoft server with access to the NetWare server and access it that way.

46. Line

Explanation: Line protocols are the transport protocols used to move data across a dial-up connection.

47. TCP/IP
NetBEUI
IPX/SPX-compatible protocol

48. A data protocol is used to package data for transport, whereas a line protocol is used to transport the data across the dial-up connection.

49. You won't need to. Although Windows NT 3.1 and 4.0 use different line protocols, Windows 95 will try PPP first anyway, so the default settings of PPP will work—they just won't be bypassed as they were before the server was upgraded.

50. Microsoft Plus

51. From the Tools menu option

52. From the Connected to X window (where X is the host that you are connected to), click on the Details button.

Explanation: With the Dialing Properties dialog box, you can set in-house dialing rules and the area code or country code to use, as well as setting credit card rules.

53. PPP

    NetWare Connect

    RAS

    SLIP

    Explanation: RAS and NetWare Connect are used for remote-access services, while SLIP and PPP are used to connect to the Internet.

54. IPX/SPX

    TCP/IP

    NetBEUI

    Explanation: A PPP connection can interoperate with a network using any of these transport protocols. Although the Internet will be using TCP/IP, other networks (such as office networks accessible via RAS) might be using other protocols.

55. You need to ensure that you have an installed modem, that you have added the dial-up adapter (Network ➢ Adapters ➢ Add ➢ Microsoft) and that you have created a connection with the Make New Connection Wizard.

    Explanation: Once Dial-up Networking is enabled, you can set up any number of different connections by only running the New Connection Wizard.

56. Broadcast Name Resolution

    HOSTS and/or LMHOSTS files

    DNS (Domain Name System) Servers

    WINS (Windows Internet Naming Service)

    Explanation: Broadcast name resolution uses NetBIOS over TCP/IP, relying on computers broadcasting their names onto the network. HOST name resolution relies on static lists of IP addresses and their corresponding computer names.

57. False

    Explanation: The dial-up server is included in the Microsoft Plus Product

58. Shiva LAN Rover

    Windows 95 dial-up server

    Windows NT Workstation, and NT Server or Windows NT Advanced Server (v. 3.1)

    Windows for Workgroups 3.11

    NetWare Connect

    Unix servers running SLIP

    Explanation: These are the networks that Dial-up Networking can connect to. For purposes of dialing in, connecting to a LAN is like connecting to the Internet.

59. True

    Explanation: This is only true with the PPP protocol, however. SLIP, the other connection protocol supplied with Windows 95, is not compressed.

60. Windows 95 has both MS Net (SMB) and NetWare (NCP) server services.

    Explanation: The SMB services are for the Microsoft network client and the NCP for the NetWare network clients.

61. False

    Explanation: You might have IP routing enabled if you're upgrading a Windows for Workgroups system to Windows 95, as WfW did support IP routing. You'll need to edit the Registry to disable this feature if it's enabled, as it will cause a Windows protection fatal error.

62. False

    Explanation: You must click on the Add button. Pressing Enter only will *not* add the address to the listing of Installed Gateways.

Sample Test

4-1   C

    Explanation: TCP/IP is the protocol used for all Internet communications, as it is stable and may be routed.

4-2   A and D

Explanation: Workgroup advertising means that a server is presented as a computer in its workgroup, while SAP advertising (used for NetWare servers) organizes all the NetWare servers together in a group at the beginning of the Entire Network listing.

4-3   A

Explanation: A single server will hold the account information for pass-through authentication. This server doesn't have to be the only one connected to, but it will be the only one storing the user accounts database.

4-4   B

Explanation: Primary domain controllers are not the only computers in a Windows NT network that validate user account information. Backup domain controllers can also take over some of the work if the PDC is overworked.

4-5   C

Explanation: WINIPCFG is an undocumented tool that allows you to find out your computer's IP address (something you won't otherwise know if your network uses a DHCP server) and other IP configuration information.

4-6   B

Explanation: The role of the WINS server is to handle name queries and resolve names. A WINS server must be a Windows NT Server machine running version 3.5 or later, as well as the WINS software.

4-7   C

Explanation: To download anything from a NetWare server, the Windows 95 client must be running the Client for NetWare Networks.

4-8   D

Explanation: You only need to specify the frame type used when you can't connect to some NetWare servers that are using a frame type other than that used by the majority.

4-9   A

Explanation: This real-mode client is the only NetWare client that supports NDS.

4-10   A

Explanation: With 0 specified for the network number, Windows 95 relies on broadcasts to determine it.

4-11   C

4-12   B and D

Explanation: DLC is not supported for DUN, and PPP is not a data protocol but a line protocol.

4-13   A and C

Explanation: Neither TCP/IP nor NetBEUI are line protocols.

4-14   A

4-15   C

Explanation: NRN is the Windows 95 version of NetWare Connect.

4-16   C

4-17   B

Explanation: As PPP is the default line protocol, you don't need to specify it, and it's the one needed to connect to a Windows NT 4.0 computer.

Unit 5 Answers

Study Questions

Monitoring System Performance

1.   NetWatcher

2. Memory Manager page outs and discards.

   Explanation: Page outs record the rate at which data is being paged to disk. A high number indicates that you're putting more data into memory than it can comfortably hold. (Some paging is, however, inevitable and does not present a problem.)

3. System Monitor

4. False

   Explanation: System Monitor only allows monitoring of IPX/SPX activity.

5. False

   Explanation: Such tools are provided with SMS (Systems Management Server). In fact, the agent can be used to provide information to any SNMP-compliant network monitoring tool.

6. True

   Explanation: NetWatcher is the tool included with Windows 95 that allows for remote and local administration of user connections on Windows 95 peer networks.

7. Select Administer and then Add Shared Folder

8. Highlight the desired folder and then either click on the Stop Sharing icon in the toolbar or select Administer and then Stop Sharing Folder.

9. Administrative

10. Thread

11. False

    Explanation: The swap file size is a function of memory management and as such is a subset of the Memory Manager category.

12. Page Outs refers to the rate at which data is paged from physical memory to disk. Page Faults describes the rate at which data required by an application is paged from disk back into physical memory.

13. Client

    Explanation: The Microsoft Client for NetWare Networks and the Microsoft Network client both record this data for their respective client types.

14. False

    Explanation: The counter for the NetWare client monitors this information but the Microsoft client's counter does not.

15. You'd use the System Monitor's Microsoft Network Monitor and choose the appropriate counter from within that category.

16. False

    Explanation: Some page faults are to be expected—they're inherent in the way that virtual memory works by permitting disk space to be used as a substitute for physical memory. However, a high rate of page faults may indicate that the demands on physical memory are too high to be optimal.

17. None of them. System Monitor doesn't track this information.

Tuning and Optimizing the System

18. MS Plus includes the System Agent that allows programs to be scheduled.

    Explanation: System Agent can technically run any application, but MS Plus comes with SA-aware versions of Defrag, ScanDisk, and the Compression Agent. System Agent is designed to simplify system maintenance.

19. True

20. ScanDisk

21. File Allocation Table (FAT), Long file names, Directory tree, DriveSpace or DoubleSpace CVF integrity, Physical Surface test, File system structure

22. Yes there is. The compression manager with Microsoft Plus uses 32KB clusters as opposed to 8KB clusters.

23. Compression Agent is a utility similar to DriveSpace, except that it achieves a greater degree of compression because of its greater cluster size and offers more discretion over the compression process.

24. Review the compression ratio for files already on your computer.

Explanation: You can determine the compression ratio by running DIR /C on the compressed volume.

25. The bitmap file can be compressed more.

Explanation: Different kinds of files can be compressed at different ratios because of their varying amounts of redundant data. Most graphics have a lot of redundant data, so they are very compressible.

26. Stop, Pause, Show Details

27. False

28. Full defragmentation, defragment files only, and consolidate free space only

29. Properties
Tools

30. HiPack
UltraPack

31. ScanDisk

32. Windows 95 supports exclusive access to a disk drive.

    Explanation: Exclusive access permits a disk utility and a user to work together so that both of them don't try to access the drive at the same time.

33. False

    Explanation: Defragmenting a disk speeds up disk access. Although defragging a disk will not free space on the disk, it will consolidate files and free space so that larger areas of free space are available, making it possible to store file data contiguously.

34. Right-click the drive's icon in My Computer, select Properties from the pop-up menu, and then select the Tools tab.

35. Although you can use other programs while defragmenting your drive, whenever the other application writes to the disk, Disk Defragmenter will restart.

    Explanation: To make the defragmenter work best, you should shut down all applications or else it will never complete. Unfortunately, this means that it may be difficult to defragment the system drive.

36. 50

    Explanation: The degree of compression you get is determined largely by the types of files you've got stored on the disk: the more compressible the files are, the more additional space you'll get. Obviously, already compressed files are not going to compress further and net more space.

37. True

38. Two

39. False

    Explanation: Any time that you ask the system to provide feedback (such as that supplied with the Details option) you're putting a strain on system resources and slowing down the process.

40. Minimize the window while it is running.

Explanation: Showing details of the disk defragmentation process results in decreased performance, as the graphical output uses system resources.

41. False

Explanation: ScanDisk bypasses the file system driver entirely.

42. Sector

Explanation: Sectors are logically grouped together to form clusters, the smallest storage unit on a disk using the FAT file system.

43. It permits disk utilities to gain exclusive access to the volume so they can perform their task without changes to the disk volume structure.

Sample Test

5-1   C

Explanation: The Advanced button in the defragmentation tool lets you choose the type of defragmentation to perform, whether to check the drive for errors, and whether you want to make these options the default.

5-2   B

5-3   B and D

5-4   D

5-5   B

5-6   A

5-7   A

Explanation: The laptop's hard disk won't be put in another computer's drive, so Ultra-Pack may be used. As the laptop is fast and hard disk space is at a premium, the first option is most appropriate for this situation.

5-8   D

5-9   B

5-10   A and D

5-11   A and B

5-12   D

5-13   A

Explanation: Defragmenting a disk reorganizes data so that all file data are grouped together, reducing read times.

Unit 6 Answers

Study Questions

Installation Failures

1. Check that you have sufficient memory.
   Check for TSRs that may be causing problems.
   Check for viruses.

2. False

   Explanation: DETCRASH.LOG is a binary file for use by the Setup program. You should examine DETLOG.TXT instead.

3. Option A will not run because Windows 95 needs a 386 or better, and option C will not run as Windows 95 can't use an EGA display.

4. Try to reconnect to the network and to the installation server.

5. `SETUPLOG.TXT`

   Explanation: `SETUPLOG.TXT` is actually for Windows 95's use, not the user's, although you can examine it to see the point at which installation halted. If the installation fails, Setup reads this file to determine which installation you must perform to complete the Setup process.

6. Windows 95 attempts to identify classes of hardware by first looking at configuration files, ROM strings, and loaded TSRs before querying hardware directly.

7. Restart Setup and select "safe recovery" when prompted to do so. You can also examine `SETUPLOG.TXT` to find out what went wrong.

8. Early Intel 386 processors (B1 stepping) have problems with 32-bit OSes. You need to replace the processor to make them work with Windows 95.

9. Disable this feature. Windows 95 Setup needs to write to the boot drive boot sector. Failure to do this may mean you have to rerun Setup.

   Explanation: The virus checker detects any attempts to write to the hard disk boot sector. Keeping it loaded may prevent Setup from running altogether, or may cause it to halt midway through.

10. `/ih`

    Explanation: This switch will force ScanDisk to run in the foreground so you can observe the results and errors of the test. For more information about the switches used with `SETUP.EXE`, see Table 2.1.

11. After ascertaining that the disk itself is working, check for viruses on the hard disk and make sure that the CMOS settings for the floppy are correct.

    Explanation: A virus on the computer may corrupt the second disk in the set because that's the one containing the user's customer information data and thus gets written to. This problem is caused by a virus on the user's computer, not on the floppy disk.

12. Viruses

Boot Process Failures

13. True

    Explanation: IO.SYS will load HIMEM.SYS if it is not in CONFIG.SYS. HIMEM.SYS is the real-mode memory manager, loaded by default.

14. True

15. The startup disk contains Windows 95 system files and utilities to allow you to boot Windows 95 if something goes wrong with your hard disk.

16. The SCSI termination. The last device in a chain must be terminated.

    Explanation: Termination is often set by jumpers on the device itself. If the removed drive was the last one in the chain, it was terminated.

Connectivity Failures

17. WINIPCFG.EXE

18. False

    Explanation: The user must have the right to remotely administer the target computer, and the target computer must have the Remote Registry service running, and the proper security must be set.

19. False

    Explanation: Windows 95 does not support IP routing, which would be necessary to route packets between networks.

20. No

    Explanation: As Windows 95 does not support routing, the network adapter connected to the LAN will not be able to hear the data sent from the Internet.

21. DHCP will only assign the first IP address. Further IP addresses will have to be manually assigned and will not be affected by DHCP leases.

22. Open the Properties sheet of the remote computer, and choose NetWatcher on the Administration tools tab.

Printer Problems

23. True

    Explanation: Some applications can only send raw printer data. In addition, if you don't have sufficient RAM to render the print job all at once, it may work better to let it be spooled as it's completed.

24. TTY.DRV

    Explanation: This support can be used to troubleshoot printing problems by simplifying the print process.

25. The memory buffers in the printer are overflowing and can't handle all the data being given them.

26. Slowly

    Explanation: Many of the solutions to memory shortages make it take longer to render the printed images, or lock up the application doing the printing.

27. When print jobs are sent to the printer, they're first rendered into an .EMF file stored in the \TEMP folder. If there's no room on the disk, then the file can't be created.

28. False

    Explanation: Even textual print jobs can be complex, as different fonts all must be stored in memory in order to be printed.

File System Problems

29. From the System Properties window, select File System and then the Troubleshooting Tab. Next, check the option Disable All 32 bit Protect-Mode Disk Drivers.

30. Nothing

Explanation: Windows 95's tunneling feature preserves long file names even when files are opened in applications that do not recognize the long names.

31. False

Explanation: Unless a real-mode driver already existed for the drive, it will be unavailable if the 32-bit drivers are disabled.

32. False

Explanation: You will only need to do this if you need to run applications that cannot work at all with long file names. This is very rare—most Win16 and DOS applications will just use the aliases.

Resource Access Problems

33. IPX network numbering

Explanation: An IPX client finds out its network number by querying the router with Router Information Protocol (RIP) requests. If the router is improperly configured, it may report the wrong number.

34. False

Explanation: In most cases, Windows 95 will detect the frame type needed and use it.

35. In the Properties for IPX/SPX-compatible protocol, in the Network applet

36. Your computer
The default gateway
A remote host computer

Explanation: You can ping your own computer with a loopback address (127.0.0.1). Pinging a computer on another network lets you determine whether you can reach the outside world. Pinging the gateway determines whether you can ping a known area on your network.

37. In the Troubleshooting tab of the file system Properties sheet (System properties sheet, Performance tab, File System button)

Explanation: By default, these options are both enabled and should remain so unless you're troubleshooting. Disabling them will impact system performance.

38. A gateway that connects to Subnet B.

39. The network is divided into at least two subnets.

Device and Device Driver Problems

40. That this particular hardware device is not functioning properly.

Explanation: The Windows 95 GUI includes several icons to show message type. This particular one signifies that the device is not functioning when it's expected to. (If the device wasn't part of the hardware profile, it just wouldn't show up in the list.)

41. False

Explanation: A disabled device will appear but will have an X through it.

Editing the Registry

42. These are backups of the Registry files that are made each time Windows 95 starts successfully.

Explanation: If anything happens to the SYSTEM.DAT or USER.DAT files that make up the Registry, the .DAO files created during the last boot will be renamed with .DAT extensions and recreate the Registry.

43. That <FILENAME>.REG contains a complete copy of the Registry.

Explanation: All keys exported from the Registry have the extension .REG, whether they're one key or the entire thing. The /c option replaces the current contents of the Registry with the contents of the specified file.

44. SYSTEM.DAT and USER.DAT compose the Registry. Both are located in the \Windows directory on local installations.

45. Values

Sample Test

6-1   C

6-2   D

6-3   D

6-4   C

Explanation: .INF files cannot be opened if there isn't enough memory. To resolve the problem, stop SmartDrive and close all applications.

6-5   A

Explanation: 127 is a loopback address. Sending a ping request to it should ping your computer.

6-6   A

6-7   C

6-8   A

Explanation: EMF increases the memory requirements for printing, as it stores the print job in printer memory before printing, which allows the print job to complete faster. All other options reduce document complexity and thus the strain on printer memory.

6-9   D

Explanation: The most likely diagnosis is that you're using the wrong printer driver, or it's been corrupted.

6-10 A and D

Explanation: A and D cannot be the default gateway address because this is a C-class network and not all of the first three quads match your's. B and C are both acceptable, even though C violates convention by not using 1 for the last quad of the default gateway.

6-11 D

Explanation: The other options check the connection to the printer and check that files may be spooled to it. Option D only reduces the complexity of the print job.

6-12 A

6-13 C

Explanation: A and B would result from a shortage of printer memory, and D will only happen if the file is not sent to the printer.

6-14 C and D

Explanation: To print with spooling (the default), there must be room on the hard disk in the temporary file directory in which to store spool files. If no room is available, the print job will fail.

6-15 A

6-16 A

Unit 7 Answers

Final Review

1. A and C

Explanation: 201.46.2.1 and 201.76.5.1 cannot be the default gateway address because this is a C-class network and not all of the first three quads match yours.

2. D

3. C

Explanation: If profiles are enabled and a user logs on who does not have a user profile, then the default user profile is used instead. The default user profile will be loaded into Jane's system Registry, into the HKEY_CURRENT_USER key.

4. C

5. D

Explanation: Like the master browser, the backup browse servers maintain lists of network resources, which they get by periodically querying the master browser. Having backup browsers reduces some of the strain on the master browser.

6. D

7. D

Explanation: Microsoft wrote the NetWare client to automatically detect the network frame type and network number, so as to save time for network administrators. Under normal circumstances, you should not have to specify the frame type, but when multiple frame types are used in a single network (e.g., when NetWare 3.11 and 4.*x* are both run in the same network) you may have to specify the frame type.

8. A

9. A

10. C

11. A

12. B and D

13. C

14. B

15. C

16. C

17. A

Explanation: A single server will hold the account information for pass-through authentication. This server doesn't have to be the only one connected to, but it will be the only one storing the user accounts database.

18. D

Explanation: Changes to a user profile are not made final until the user logs off. When two instances of a user account are opened at once, then no changes are finalized until the last instance is closed. Any changes made to the instance closed first are not saved.

19. B

20. C

21. C

Explanation: WINIPCFG is an undocumented tool that allows you to find out your computer's IP address (something you won't otherwise know if your network uses a DHCP server) and other IP configuration information.

22. B

23. B

24. C

Explanation: The Advanced button in the defragmentation tool lets you choose the type of defragmentation to perform, whether to check the drive for errors, and whether you want to make these options the default.

25. B

26. C

27. A

Explanation: Virtual memory is a combined total of physical memory (the amount of RAM installed) and an area on the hard disk used to store data not immediately being used. It takes less time to retrieve data from RAM than from the hard disk. When data is retrieved from the storage place on the hard disk and reinstalled into physical memory, this is called a *page fault*. An excess of page faults indicates there is not enough room in RAM for all the data that the user is trying to store and make accessible quickly. Page faults can be reduced with more RAM.

28. A

29. B

Explanation: As you're compressing data on a Zip drive, it's possible that the compressed data may need to be read from another system (otherwise, you'd probably just be storing it on your hard disk and compressing that). UltraPack compression cannot be read with Windows 95, but HiPack can.

30. D

31. A

32. D

Explanation: 127.0.0.1 is a loopback address. Sending a ping request to it will ping your computer.

33. C and D

Explanation: Reducing the number of fonts and graphical elements will not affect print speed, although it may affect the document's appearance if you're experiencing memory shortages. A and B both speed up the printing process.

34. A

35. D

36. A

Explanation: Only one real-mode network client can run at a time as they're not aware of other clients and would not cooperate with each other.

37. A and D

Explanation: Workgroup advertising means that a server is presented as a computer in its workgroup, while SAP advertising (used for NetWare servers) organizes all the NetWare servers together in a group at the beginning of the Entire Network listing. SAP would be required for non-Windows 95 Novell clients to see the shared resource.

38. A

39. D

Explanation: The Client for Microsoft Networks is a protected-mode client, and as such uses no conventional memory.

40. A and B

Explanation: Mandatory user profiles stored on the server will give *all* users the same settings to use, so those settings will apply no matter which machine they're logging in from. System policies will be automatically downloaded from the primary domain controller to the client. Mandatory user profiles are more perfectly restrictive than system policies, but in both cases the settings will follow the users and make them follow your guidelines.

41. D

Explanation: The option is not unavailable when grayed out, but you can't tell from looking at it whether it's enabled or disabled. The gray box means only that it's using the same settings that it was the last time you edited the policy.

42. D

Explanation: System policies must be loaded from the server, not from the local machine.

43. A

Explanation: DLC is required to transfer data to printers connected directly to the network, rather than to a server.

44. A and B

Explanation: Hide share passwords with asterisks is currently disabled, so you need to click this option's checkbox to enable it. You can't tell whether the Disable password caching option is enabled, so you need to check it. The other two options aren't relevant to the discussion—it's unimportant whether they get checked.

45. C

46. C

47. D

Explanation: You're using share-level permissions on your computer, so group and user rights aren't relevant. C only hides the share. D is the only option that allows you to distinguish between users when using share-level permissions.

48. D

49. A and B

Explanation: User profile information, mandatory or discretionary, is stored in each user's Mail directory. System policy information is stored in the Sys\Public directory of the preferred server.

50. A

Explanation: NETX is the only real-mode networking client that will work with NetWare 3.12. VLM is for connecting to NetWare 4.x servers, and the Client for NetWare Networks is a protected-mode client. NWCON doesn't exist.

51. B and D

Explanation: Client for NetWare Networks is faster than the real-mode clients and supports bindery services. Only real-mode NetWare clients support NDS and NetWare IP, however.

52. C

Explanation: Each workgroup has its own master browser, and each protocol has a master browser.

53. B

Explanation: DNS is the Domain Name Service. DHCP is used for dynamic allocation of IP addresses, and WINS resolves NetBIOS names to IP addresses. RFC is short for Request for Comment and is a technical description of a service.

54. B

55. C

Explanation: Fully qualified domain names name the machine host name and domain name.

56. D

Explanation: The secondary DNS server is only queried if the first one does not respond at all, so if the first one worked a second query will not be attempted. WINS would not be queried for a fully qualified domain name.

57. A

58. B

Explanation: When you join the network, your workstation sends a RIP broadcast to ascertain the frame type in common use on the network. You need to specify the frame type used when you can't connect to some NetWare servers that are using a frame type other than that used by the majority.

59. A

Explanation: The VLM real-mode client is the only NetWare client that supports NDS. However, it cannot be used to access user profiles.

60. C

61. B and D

Explanation: DLC is not supported for DUN (or for NT-Windows 95 networking, for that matter), and PPP is not a data protocol but a line protocol.

62. A and C

Explanation: Neither TCP/IP nor NetBEUI are line protocols.

63. A

64. D

Explanation: NRN is the line protocol Windows 95 version of NetWare Connect and should be used for dialing up to a NetWare server. IPX/SPX is not a line protocol, but a data protocol (as is TCP/IP).

65. C

66. C

Explanation: As PPP is the default line protocol, you don't need to specify it, and it's the one needed to connect to a Windows NT 4.0 computer. The Client for Microsoft Networks must already be installed if the computer is part of a Windows 95 network.

67. D

Explanation: You only need to specify an IP address when no Dynamic Host Configuration Protocol (DHCP) server (or other address-leasing service) is available to supply you with an IP address.

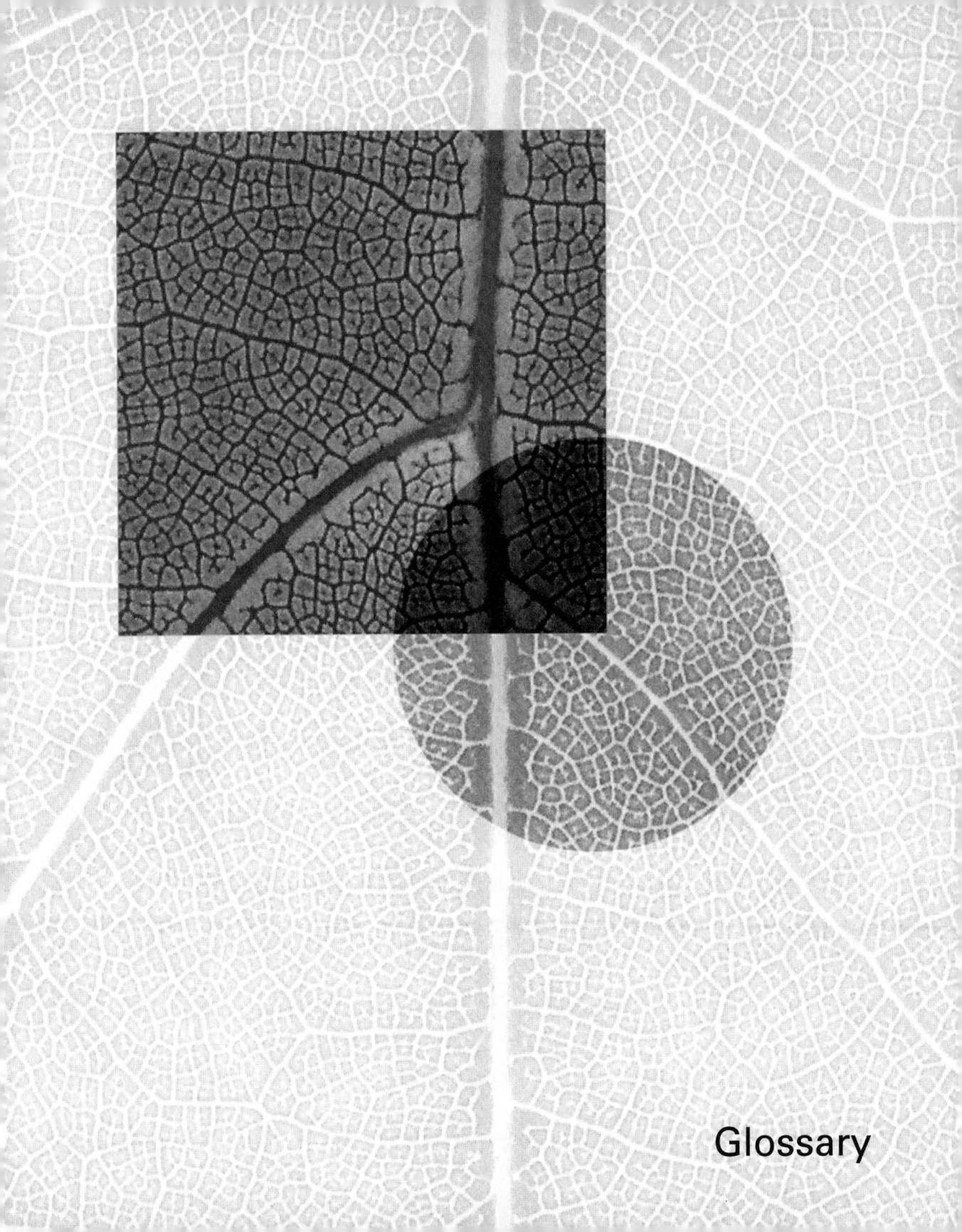

Glossary

Accounts   Containers for security identifiers, passwords, permissions, group associations, and preferences for each user of a system. The User Manager for Domains utility is used to administer accounts. See also *Security Identifiers, Preferences, Permissions, Groups.*

Adapter   Any hardware device that allows communications to occur through physically dissimilar systems. This term usually refers to peripheral cards permanently mounted inside computers that provide an interface from the computer's bus to another media such as a hard disk or a network. See also *Network Interface Card, Small Computer Systems Interface.*

Administrators   Users who are part of the Administrators group. This group has the ultimate set of security permissions. See also *Permissions, Groups.*

Application Layer   The layer of the OSI model that interfaces with user-mode programs, called *applications,* by providing high-level network services based upon lower-level network layers. Network file systems like Named Pipes are an example of application layer software. See also *Named Pipes, Open Systems Interconnect Model.*

Application Programming Interface (API)   A standard set of API calls is to allow transparent access to operating system or networking functions.

Asynchronous Data Stream   Packets of information are passed one packet at a time rather than several packets in a synchronized burst. Resources can be physical like your modem, or logical like a fax service on your computer that utilizes the modem for the transmittal and reception of faxes.

Backup Browser   A computer on a Microsoft network that maintains a list of computers and services available on the network. The master browser supplies this list. The backup browser distributes the Browsing service load to a workgroup or domain. See also *Master Browser.*

Backup Domain Controllers   Servers that contain accurate replications of the security and user databases; servers can authenticate workstations if the primary domain controller does not respond or is overloaded. See also *Primary Domain Controller.*

Basic Input/Output System (BIOS)   A set of routines in firmware that provides the most basic software interface drivers for hardware attached to the computer. The BIOS contains the bootstrap routine. See also *Boot, Driver.*

Bindery   A NetWare structure that contains user accounts and permissions. It is similar to the Security Accounts Manager in Windows NT. See also *Security Accounts Manager.*

BIOS   See *Basic Input/Output System.*

Boot   The process of loading a computer's operating system. Booting usually occurs in multiple phases, each successively more complex until the entire operating system and all its services are running. Also called *bootstrap.* The computer's BIOS must contain the first level of booting. See also *Basic Input/Output System.*

Bridge   A device that connects two networks of the same data link protocol by forwarding packets destined for computers on the other side of the bridge. See also *Router, Data Link Layer.*

Browser   A computer on a Microsoft network that maintains a list of computers and services available on the network.

Browsing   The process of requesting the list of shared resources on a network from a browser.

Caching   A speed optimization technique that keeps a copy of the most recently used data in a fast, high-cost, low-capacity storage device rather than in the device upon which the actual data resides. Caching assumes that recently used data is likely to be used again. Fetching data from the cache is faster than fetching data from the slower, larger storage device. Most caching algorithms also copy next-most-likely-to-be-used data and perform write caching to further increase speed gains. See also *Write-Back Caching, Write-through Caching.*

Client   A computer on a network that subscribes to the services provided by a server. See also *Server.*

Client/Server   A network architecture that dedicates certain computers called *servers* to act as service providers to computers called *clients*, which users operate to perform work. Servers can be dedicated to providing one or more network service such as file storage, shared printing, communications, e-mail service, and Web response. See also *Share, Peer*.

Client/Server Applications   Applications that split large applications into two components: computer-intensive processes that run on application servers and user interfaces that run on clients. Client/server applications communicate over the network through interprocess communication mechanisms. See also *Client, Server, Interprocess Communications*.

Code   Synonymous with *software* but used when the software is the object of discussion, rather than the utility it provides.

Components   Interchangeable elements of a complex software or hardware system. See also *Module*.

Compression   A space-optimization scheme that reduces the size (length) of a data set by exploiting the fact that most useful data contains a great deal of redundancy. Compression reduces redundancy by creating symbols smaller than the data they represent and an index that defines the value of the symbols for each compressed set of data.

Computer Name   A 1- to 15-character NetBIOS name used to uniquely identify a computer on the network. See also *Network Basic Input/Output System*.

Control Panel   A Windows interface that provides access to applets controlling the function of specific operating system tasks. The Registry contains the Control Panel settings on a system and/or per-user basis. See also *Registry, Accounts*.

Cooperative Multitasking   A multitasking scheme in which each process must voluntarily return time to a central scheduling route. If any single process fails to return to the central scheduler, the computer will lock up. Both Windows and the Macintosh operating systems use this scheme. See also *Preemptive Multitasking, Windows for Workgroups.*

Data Link Layer   In the OSI model, the layer that provides the digital interconnection of network devices and the software that directly operates these devices, such as network interface adapters. See also *Physical Layer, Network Layer, Open Systems Interconnect Model.*

Database   A related set of data organized by type and purpose. The term can also include the application software that manipulates the data. The Windows 95 Registry is a database. See also *Registry.*

Desktop   A directory that the background of the Windows Explorer shell represents. By default, the Desktop contains objects that contain the local storage devices and available network shares. Also a key operating part of the Windows GUI. See also *Explorer, Shell.*

DHCP   See *Dynamic Host Configuration Protocol.*

Dial-up Connections   Data link layer digital connections made via modems over telephone lines. The term *dial-up* refers to temporary digital connections, as opposed to leased telephone lines, which provide permanent connections. See also *Data Link Layer, Public Switched Telephone Network.*

DNS   See *Domain Name Service.*

Domain   In Microsoft networks a domain is an arrangement of client and server computers referenced by a specific name that share a single security permissions database. On the Internet a domain is a named collection of hosts and subdomains, registered with a unique name by the InterNIC. See also *Workgroup, InterNIC.*

Domain Controllers Servers that authenticate workstation network logon requests by comparing a username and password against account information stored in the user accounts database. A user cannot access a domain without authentication from a domain controller. See also *Primary Domain Controller, Backup Domain Controllers, Domain*.

Domain Name The textual identifier of a specific Internet host. Domain names are in the form *server.organization.type* (www.microsoft.com) and are resolved to Internet addresses by domain name servers. See also *Domain Name Server*.

Domain Name Server An Internet host dedicated to the function of translating fully qualified domain names into IP addresses. See also *Domain Name*.

Domain Name Service (DNS) The TCP/IP network service that translates host names into numerical Internet network addresses. See also *Transmission Control Protocol/Internet Protocol, Internet*.

Driver A program that provides a software interface to a hardware device. Drivers are written for the specific device they control, but they present a common software interface to the computer's operating system, allowing all devices (of a similar type) to be controlled as if they were the same. See also *Data Link Layer, Operating System*.

Dual-Booting Windows 95 allows you to boot to another operating system. This can be a previous version of DOS, Windows, or Windows NT.

Dynamic Data Exchange (DDE) A method of interprocess communication within the Microsoft Windows operating systems.

Dynamic Host Configuration Protocol (DHCP) A method of automatically assigning IP addresses to client computers on a network.

Dynamic Link Libraries (DLL) Modular functions that can be used by many programs simultaneously. There are hundreds of functions stored within DLLs.

Easter Eggs   A mini application that is normally undocumented but built into many applications.

ECP   See *Extended Capabilities Port*.

Electronic Mail (E-Mail)   A type of client/server application that provides a routed, stored-message service between any two user e-mail accounts. E-mail accounts are not the same as user accounts, but a one-to-one relationship usually exists between them. See also *Internet*.

Emergency Repair Disk   A floppy diskette created by the RDISK.EXE program that contains critical Registry information about a Windows 95 installation. With an emergency repair disk, a Windows 95 installation can be salvaged using the restore option when reinstalling from CD-ROM. See also *Registry*.

Encryption   The process of obscuring information by modifying it according to a mathematical function known only to the intended recipient. Encryption secures information being transmitted over non-secure or untrusted media. See also *Security*.

Enterprise Network   A complex network consisting of multiple servers and multiple domains over a large geographic area.

Environment Variables   Variables, such as the search path, that contain information available to programs and batch files about the current operating system environment.

Ethernet   The most popular data link layer standard for local area networking. Ethernet implements the carrier sense multiple access with collision detection (CSMA/CD) method of arbitrating multiple computer access to the same network. This standard supports the use of Ethernet over any type of media including wireless broadcast. Standard Ethernet operates as 10 megabits per second. Fast Ethernet operates at 100 megabits per second. See also *Data Link Layer*.

Exchange   Microsoft's messaging application. Exchange implements Microsoft's mail application programming interface (MAPI) as well as other messaging protocols such as POP, SNMP, and faxing to provide a flexible message composition and reception service. See also *Electronic Mail*.

Explorer   The default shell for Windows 95 and Windows NT 4.0. Explorer implements the more flexible Desktop object paradigm rather than the Program Manager paradigm used in earlier versions of Windows. See also *Desktop*.

Extended Capabilities Port (ECP)   ECP allows you to add additional printer cards to your PC. The additional cards will become ECPs and can be used to attach a printer.

FAT   See *File Allocation Table*.

File Allocation Table (FAT)   The file system used by MS-DOS and available to other operating systems such as Windows (all variations), OS/2, and the Macintosh. FAT has become something of a mass storage compatibility standard because of its simplicity and wide availability. FAT has few fault tolerance features and can become corrupted through normal use over time. See also *File System*.

File Attributes   Bits that show the status of a file (for example, archived, hidden, read-only) are stored along with the name and location of a file in a directory entry. Different operating systems use different file attributes to implement such services as sharing, compression, and security.

File System   A software component that manages the storage of files on a mass storage device by providing services that can create, read, write, and delete files. File systems impose an ordered database of files, called volumes, on the mass storage device. Volumes use hierarchies of directories to organize files. See also *Volume, Database*.

File Transfer Protocol (FTP)   A simple Internet protocol that transfers complete files from an FTP server to a client running the FTP client. FTP provides a simple method of transferring files between computers but cannot perform browsing functions. You must know the address of the FTP server to which you want to attach. See also *Internet, Uniform Resource Locator*.

Frame Type   Main parameter of IPX/SPX protocol. There are different frame types that can be run on your network. A frame can be considered a dialect—Ethernet has four possible frames or dialects, and Token Ring has two possible frame types.

FTP   See *File Transfer Protocol.*

Gateway   A computer that serves as a router, a format translator, or a security filter for an entire network or subnet.

GDI   See *Graphical Device Interface.*

General Protection Faults   A general protection fault occurs when a program violates the integrity of the system. This often happens when a program tries to access memory that is not part of its memory address space. This GP Fault is a defense mechanism employed by the operating system.

Graphical Device Interface (GDI)   The programming interface and graphical services provided to Win32 for programs to interact with graphical devices such as the screen and printer. See also *Programming Interfaces, Win32.*

Graphical User Interface (GUI)   A computer shell program that represents mass storage devices, directories, and files as graphical objects on a screen. A cursor driven by a pointing device such as a mouse manipulates the objects. Typically, icons that can be opened into windows that show the data contained by the object represent the objects. See also *Shell, Explorer.*

Groups   Security entities to which users can be assigned membership for the purpose of applying the broad set of group permissions to the user. By managing permissions for groups and assigning users to groups, rather than assigning permissions to users, security administrators can keep coherent control of very large security environments. See also *Permissions, Accounts, Security, Local Group.*

GUI   See *Graphical User Interface.*

Hardware Profiles   Used to manage portable computers that have different configurations based on their location.

Home Directory   A directory that stores user's personal files and programs.

Home Page   The default page returned by an HTTP server when a URL containing no specific document is requested. See also *Hypertext Transfer Protocol, Uniform Resource Locator.*

Host   An Internet server. Hosts are constantly connected to the Internet. See also *Internet.*

HTML   See *Hypertext Markup Language.*

HTTP   See *Hypertext Transfer Protocol.*

Hyperlink   A link in text or graphics files that have a Web address embedded within them. By clicking on the link, you jump to another Web address. You can identify a hyperlink because it is usually underlined or a different color from the rest of the Web page. See also *World Wide Web.*

Hypertext Markup Language (HTML)   A textual data format that identifies sections of a document as headers, lists, hypertext links, and so on. HTML is the data format used on the World Wide Web for the publication of Web pages. See also *Hypertext Transfer Protocol, World Wide Web.*

Hypertext Transfer Protocol (HTTP)   Hypertext transfer protocol is an Internet protocol that transfers HTML documents over the Internet and responds to context changes that happen when a user clicks on a hypertext link. See also *Hypertext Markup Language, World Wide Web.*

IDE   A simple mass storage device interconnection bus that operates at 5Mbps and can handle no more than two attached devices. IDE devices are similar to but less expensive than SCSI devices. See also *Small Computer Systems Interface.*

IIS   See *Internet Information Server.*

Industry Standard Architecture (ISA) The design standard for 16-bit Intel compatible motherboards and peripheral buses. The 32/64-bit PCI bus standard is replacing the ISA standard. Adapters and interface cards must conform to the bus standard(s) used by the motherboard in order to be used with a computer.

Integrated Services Digital Network (ISDN) A direct, digital dial-up PSTN data link layer connection that operates at 64KB per channel over regular twisted-pair cable between a subscriber site and a PSTN central office. ISDN provides twice the data rate of the fastest modems per channel. Up to 24 channels can be multiplexed over two twisted pairs. See also *Public Switched Telephone Network, Data Link Layer.*

Internet A voluntarily interconnected global network of computers based upon the TCP/IP protocol suite. TCP/IP was originally developed by the U.S. Department of Defense's Advanced Research Projects Agency to facilitate the interconnection of military networks and was provided free to universities. The obvious utility of worldwide digital network connectivity and the availability of free complex networking software developed at universities doing military research attracted other universities, research institutions, private organizations, businesses, and finally the individual home user. The Internet is now available to all current commercial computing platforms. See also *File Transfer Protocol, World Wide Web, Transmission Control Protocol/Internet Protocol.*

Internet Explorer A World Wide Web browser produced by Microsoft and included free with Windows 95 and Windows NT 4.0. See also *World Wide Web, Internet.*

Internet Information Server (IIS) Serves Internet higher-level protocols like HTTP and FTP to clients using Web browsers. See also *Hypertext Transfer Protocol, File Transfer Protocol,* and *World Wide Web.*

Internet Protocol (IP) The network layer protocol upon which the Internet is based. IP provides a simple connectionless packet exchange. See also *Transmission Control Protocol/Internet Protocol, Internet.*

Internet Service Provider (ISP)   A company that provides dial-up connections to the Internet. See also *Internet*.

Internetwork Packet Exchange (IPX)   The network protocol developed by Novell for its NetWare product. IPX is a routable protocol similar to IP but much easier to manage and with lower communication overhead. The term IPX can also refer to the family of protocols that includes the Synchronous Packet Exchange (SPX) transport layer protocol, a connection-oriented protocol that guarantees delivery in order, similar to the service provided by TCP. See also *Internet Protocol, NetWare*.

InterNIC   The agency responsible for assigning IP addresses. See also *Internet Protocol, IP Address*.

Interprocess Communications (IPC)   A generic term describing any manner of client/server communication protocol, specifically those operating in the session, presentation, and application layers. Interprocess communications mechanisms provide a method for the client and server to trade information. See also *Named Pipes, Remote Procedure Calls, Network Basic Input/Output System, Network Dynamic Data Exchange*.

Interrupt Request (IRQ)   A hardware signal from a peripheral device to the microcomputer indicating that it has I/O traffic to send. If the microprocessor is not running a more important service, it will interrupt its current activity and handle the interrupt request. IBM PCs have 16 levels of interrupt request lines. Under Windows NT each device must have a unique interrupt request line. See also *Microprocessor*.

Intranet   A privately owned network based on the TCP/IP protocol suite. See also *Transmission Control Protocol/Internet Protocol*.

IP   See *Internet Protocol*.

IP Address   A four-byte (32-bit) number that uniquely identifies a computer on an IP internetwork. InterNIC assigns the first bytes of Internet IP addresses and administers them in hierarchies. Huge organizations like the government or top-level ISPs have class A addresses, large organizations and most ISPs have class B addresses, and small companies have class C addresses. In a class A address, InterNIC assigns the first byte, and the owning organization assigns the remaining three bytes. In a class B address, InterNIC or the higher-level ISP assigns the first two bytes, and the organization assigns the remaining two bytes. In a class C address, InterNIC or the higher-level ISP assigns the first three bytes, and the organization assigns the remaining byte. Organizations not attached to the Internet are free to assign IP addresses as they please for internal use. See also *Internet Protocol, Internet, InterNIC.*

IPC   See *Interprocess Communications.*

IPX   See *Internetwork Packet Exchange.*

IRQ   See *Interrupt Request.*

ISA   See *Industry Standard Architecture.*

ISDN   See *Integrated Services Digital Network.*

ISP   See *Internet Service Provider.*

Kernel   The core process of a preemptive operating system, consisting of a multitasking scheduler and the basic services that provide security. Depending on the operating system, other services such as virtual memory drivers may be built into the Kernel. The Kernel is responsible for managing the scheduling of threads and processes. See also *Operating System, Driver.*

LAN Manager   The Microsoft brand of a network product jointly developed by IBM and Microsoft that provided an early client/server environment. LAN Manager/Server was eclipsed by NetWare, but it was the genesis of many important protocols and IPC mechanisms used today, such as NetBIOS, Named Pipes, and NetBEUI. Portions of this product exist today in OS/2 Warp Server. See also *Interprocess Communications.*

LAN Server   The IBM brand of a network product jointly developed by IBM and Microsoft. See also *LAN Manager.*

Local User Profiles   Local profiles are stored only on the local computer. If a user logs onto one computer, makes changes to the environment, and then logs onto another computer, the changes from the first computer are not reflected on the second computer.

Local Group   A group that exists in an NT computer's local accounts database. Local groups can reside on NT Workstations or NT Servers and can contain users or global groups.

Logging   The process of recording information about activities and errors in the operating system.

Logon Script   Command files that automate the logon process by performing utility functions such as attaching to additional server resources or automatically running different programs based upon the user account that established the logon.

Long File Name (LFN)   A file name longer than the eight characters plus three-character extension allowed by MS-DOS. In Windows NT and Windows 95, file names can contain up to 255 characters.

Mandatory User Profile   A profile that is created by an administrator and saved with a special extension (.MAN) so that the user cannot modify the profile in any way. Mandatory user profiles can be assigned to a single user or a group of users. See also *User Profile*.

MAPI   See *Messaging Application Programming Interface*.

Master Boot Record   After the BIOS Bootstrap the system then loads the Master Boot Record (MBR) and the partition table of the bootable drive, and executes the MBR.

Master Browser   The computer on a network that maintains a list of computers and services available on the network and distributes the list to other browsers. The master browser may also promote potential browsers to be browsers. See also *Browser, Browsing, Backup Browser*.

Media Access Control (MAC)   The data link layer or MAC consists of the driver for the network card. This layer helps watch for errors in the transmission and conversion of signals.

Messaging Application Programming Interface (MAPI)   Messaging application standard developed by Microsoft to allow for interaction between an application and various message service providers.

Metafiles   Windows metafiles (*.WMF) are files that contain the Windows internal graphics language. These metafiles are basically a collection of internal commands that Windows 95 uses to render graphics to the screen.

Microprocessor   An integrated semiconductor circuit designed to automatically perform lists of logical and arithmetic operations. Modern microprocessors independently manage memory pools and support multiple instruction lists called *threads*. Microprocessors are also capable of responding to interrupt requests from peripherals and include onboard support for complex floating-point arithmetic. Microprocessors must have instructions when they are first powered on. These instructions are contained in nonvolatile firmware called a BIOS. See also *Basic Input/Output System, Operating System*.

MIDI   See *Musical Instrument Digital Interface*.

Module   A software component of a modular operating system that provides a certain defined service. Modules can be installed or removed depending upon the service requirements of the software running on the computer. Modules allow operating systems and applications to be customized to fit the needs of the user.

MPR   See *MultiProtocol Router*.

Multiprocessing   Using two or more processors simultaneously to perform a computing task. Depending on the operating system, processing may be done asymmetrically, wherein certain processors are assigned certain threads independent of the load they create, or symmetrically, wherein threads are dynamically assigned to processors according to an equitable scheduling scheme. The term usually describes a multiprocessing capacity built into the computer at a hardware level in that the computer itself supports more than one processor. However, *multiprocessing* can also be applied to network computing applications achieved through interprocess communication mechanisms. Client/server applications are, in fact, examples of multiprocessing. See also *Interprocess Communications*.

MultiProtocol Router (MPR)   Services included with NT Server that allow you to route traffic between IPX and TCP/IP subnets. MPR also allows you to facilitate DHCP requests and forward BOOTP relay agents. See also *Internetwork Packet Exchange, Transmission Control Protocol/Internet Protocol, Dynamic Host Configuration Protocol.*

Multitasking   The capacity of an operating system to rapidly switch among threads of execution. Multitasking allows processor time to be divided among threads as if each thread ran on its own slower processor. Multitasking operating systems allow two or more applications to run at the same time and can provide a greater degree of service to applications than single-tasking operating systems like MS-DOS. See also *Multiprocessing, Multithreaded.*

Multithreaded   Multithreaded refers to programs that have more than one chain of execution, thus relying on the services of a multitasking or multiprocessing operating system to operate. Multiple chains of execution allow programs to simultaneously perform more than one task. In multitasking computers, multithreading is merely a convenience used to make programs run smoother and free the program from the burden of switching between tasks itself. On multiprocessing computers, multithreading allows the compute burden of the program to be spread across many processors. Programs that are not multithreaded cannot take advantage of multiple processors in a computer. See also *Multitasking, Multiprocessing.*

Musical Instrument Digital Interface (MIDI)   A serial interface standard that allows you to connect musical instruments to the computer.

Named Pipes   An interprocess communication mechanism that is implemented as a file system service, allowing programs to be modified to run on it without using a proprietary application programming interface. Named Pipes were developed to support more robust client/server communications than those allowed by the simpler NetBIOS. See also *Interprocess Communications.*

NCP   See *NetWare Core Protocol.*

NDIS   See *Network Driver Interface Specification.*

NDS   See *NetWare Directory Services.*

NetWatcher Interactive tool for creating, controlling, and monitoring remote shared resources.

NetBEUI See *NetBIOS Extended User Interface.*

NetBIOS See *Network Basic Input/Output System.*

NetBIOS Extended User Interface (NetBEUI) A simple network layer transport developed to support NetBIOS applications. NetBEUI is not routable, and so it is not appropriate for larger networks. NetBEUI is the fastest transport protocol available for Windows 95.

NetBIOS Gateway A service provided by RAS that allows NetBIOS requests to be forwarded independent of transport protocol. For example, NetBIOS requests from a remote computer connected via NetBEUI can be sent over the network via NWLink. See also *Network Basic Input/Output System, NetBIOS over TCP/IP, NetBIOS Extended User Interface.*

NetBIOS over TCP/IP (NetBT) A network service that implements the NetBIOS IPC over the TCP/IP protocol stack. See also *Network Basic Input/Output System, Interprocess Communications, Transmission Control Protocol/Internet Protocol.*

NetBT See *NetBIOS over TCP/IP.*

NetDDE See *Network Dynamic Data Exchange.*

NetSetup NetSetup uses the Policy Editor interface to configure setup scripts. You can also specify a setup server.

NetWare A popular network operating system developed by Novell in the early 1980s. NetWare is a cooperative, multitasking, highly optimized, dedicated-server network operating system that has client support for most major operating systems. Recent versions of NetWare include graphical client tools for management from client stations. At one time, NetWare accounted for more than 70 percent of the network operating system market. See also *Windows NT.*

NetWare Core Protocol (NCP)   NetWare servers communicate using a language called NCP. By installing the Client for NetWare, you enable Windows 95 to communicate with NetWare servers.

NetWare Directory Services (NDS)   In NetWare a distributed hierarchy of network services such as servers, shared volumes, and printers. NetWare implements NDS as a directory structure having elaborate security and administration mechanisms. See also *NetWare.*

Network Basic Input/Output System (NetBIOS)   A client/server interprocess communication service developed by IBM in the early 1980s. NetBIOS presents a relatively primitive mechanism for communication in client/server applications, but its widespread acceptance and availability across most operating systems makes it a logical choice for simple network applications. Many of the network IPC mechanisms in Windows NT are implemented over NetBIOS. See also *Interprocess Communications, Client/Server.*

Network Driver Interface Specification (NDIS)   A Microsoft specification to which network adapter drivers must conform in order to work with Microsoft network operating systems. NDIS provides a many-to-many binding between network adapter drivers and transport protocols. See also *Transport Protocol.*

Network Dynamic Data Exchange (NetDDE)   An interprocess communication mechanism developed by Microsoft to support the distribution of DDE applications over a network. See also *Interprocess Communications, Dynamic Data Exchange.*

Network Interface Card (NIC)   A physical layer adapter device that allows a computer to connect to and communicate over a local area network. See also *Ethernet, Token Ring, Adapter.*

Network Layer   The layer of the OSI model that creates a communication path between two computers via routed packets. Transport protocols implement both the network layer and the transport layer of the OSI stack. IP is a network layer service. See also *Internet Protocol, Transport Protocol, Open Systems Interconnect Model.*

Network Operating System   A computer operating system specifically designed to optimize a computer's ability to respond to service requests. Servers run network operating systems. Windows NT Server and NetWare are both network operating systems. See also *Windows NT, Server, NetWare.*

Network User   A user who logs on to the network using the SAM from a remote domain controller.

New Technology File System (NTFS)   A secure, transaction-oriented file system developed for Windows NT that incorporates the Windows NT security model for assigning permissions and shares. NTFS is optimized for hard drives larger than 500MB and requires too much overhead to be used on hard disk drives smaller than 50MB.

Non-browser   A computer on a network that will not maintain a list of other computers and services on the network. See also *Browser, Browsing.*

NTFS   See *New Technology File System.*

Open Graphics Language (OpenGL)   A standard interface for the presentation of two- and three-dimensional visual data.

Open Systems Interconnect Model (OSI Model)   A model for network component interoperability developed by the International Standards Organization to promote cross-vendor compatibility of hardware and software network systems. The OSI model splits the process of networking into seven distinct services. Each layer uses the services of the layer below to provide its service to the layer above. See also *Physical Layer, Data Link Layer, Network Layer, Transport Layer, Session Layer, Presentation Layer, Application Layer.*

OpenGL See also *Open Graphics Language*.

Operating System A collection of services that form a foundation upon which applications run. Operating systems may be simple I/O service providers with a command shell, such as MS-DOS, or they may be sophisticated, preemptive, multitasking applications platforms such as Windows 95. See also *Network Operating System, Preemptive Multitasking, Kernel*.

Optimization Any effort to reduce the workload on a hardware component by eliminating, obviating, or reducing the amount of work required of the hardware component through any means. For instance, file caching is an optimization that reduces the workload of a hard disk drive.

OSI Model See *Open Systems Interconnect Model*.

OSR2 New versions of Windows 95 include the B or OSR2 release, which have various features added.

Page File See *Swap File*.

Partition A section of a hard disk that can contain an independent file system volume. Partitions can be used to keep multiple operating systems and file systems on the same hard disk. See also *Volume*.

PCI See *Peripheral Connection Interface*.

PDC See *Primary Domain Controller*.

Peer A networked computer that both shares resources with other computers and accesses the shared resources of other computers. A nondedicated server. See also *Server, Client*.

Peer-to-Peer In Windows 95, peer-to-peer refers to peer-to-peer network or peer-to-peer type messaging. In either case, it is able to be configured and used by end users with no particular need for an administrator to do anything on the server. Each node is administered by its user.

Peripheral Connection Interface (PCI)   A high-speed 32/64-bit bus interface developed by Intel and widely accepted as the successor to the 16-bit ISA interface. PCI devices support I/O throughput about 40 times faster than the ISA bus.

Permissions   Assignments of levels of access to a resource made to groups or users.

Security constructs that regulate access to resources by user name or group affiliation. Administrators can assign permissions to allow any level of access, such as read only, read/write, delete, by controlling the ability of users to initiate object services. Security is implemented by checking the user's security identifier against each object's access control list. See also *Security Identifiers*.

Physical Layer   The cables, connectors, and connection ports of a network. The passive physical components required to create a network. See also *Open Systems Interconnect Model*.

Plug and Play   This technology allows you to install Plug-and-Play hardware into your system without having to reconfigure the hardware or the computer system. When you add a new Plug-and-Play device, Windows 95 will automatically detect and configure the device.

Point and Print   Used to install driver files for a networked printer by dragging the Point-and-Print printer icon from the networked PC to the Printers folder. Documents can be printed to networking printers by simply dragging and dropping onto the printer icon.

Point-to-Point Protocol (PPP)   A data link layer transport that performs over point-to-point network connections such as serial or modem lines. PPP can negotiate any transport protocol used by both systems involved in the link and can automatically assign IP, DNS, and gateway addresses when used with TCP/IP. See also *Internet Protocol, Domain Name Service, Gateway*.

Point-to-Point Tunneling Protocol (PPTP)   Protocol used to create secure connections between private networks through the public Internet or an ISP. See also *Internet, Internet Service Provider*.

PPI See *Print Provider Interface.*

PPP See *Point-to-Point Protocol.*

PPTP See *Point-to-Point Tunneling Protocol.*

Preemptive Multitasking A multitasking implementation in which an interrupt routine in the Kernel manages the scheduling of processor time among running threads. The threads themselves do not need to support multitasking in any way because the microprocessor will preempt the thread with an interrupt, save its state, update all thread priorities according to its scheduling algorithm, and pass control to the highest priority thread awaiting execution. See also *Kernel, Thread, Operating System.*

Preferences Characteristics of user accounts, such as password, profile location, home directory, and logon script.

Presentation Layer That layer of the OSI model that converts and translates (if necessary) information between the session and application layers. See also *Open Systems Interconnect Model.*

Primary Domain Controller (PDC) The NT domain server that contains the master copy of the security, computer, and user accounts databases and that can authenticate workstations. The PDC can replicate its databases to one or more backup domain controllers. The PDC is usually also the master browser for the domain. See also *Backup Domain Controllers, Domain, Master Browser.*

Print Driver Each printing device has its own command set. The print driver is the specific software that understands your print device. Each print device has an associated print driver.

Print Provider Interface The Print Provider Interface is a modular interface with interchangeable components which allows third-party vendors to seamlessly integrate network print drivers into Windows 95.

Print Server   Print servers are the computers on which the printers have been defined. When you send a job to a network printer not connected directly to the network, you are actually sending it to the print server first.

Print Spooler (Print Queue)   The print spooler is a directory or folder on the print server that actually stores the print jobs until they can be printed. It's very important that your print server and print spooler have enough hard disk space to hold all of the print jobs that could be pending at any given time. See also *Print Server*.

Priority   A level of execution importance assigned to a thread. In combination with other factors, the priority level determines how often that thread will get computer time according to a scheduling algorithm. See also *Preemptive Multitasking*.

Process   A running program containing one or more threads. A process encapsulates the protected memory and environment for its threads.

Processor   A circuit designed to automatically perform lists of logical and arithmetic operations. Unlike microprocessors, processors may be designed from discrete components rather than be a monolithic integrated circuit. See also *Microprocessor*.

Program   A list of processor instructions designed to perform a certain function. A running program is called a *process*. A package of one or more programs and attendant data designed to meet a certain application is called *software*. See also *Microprocessor*.

Programming Interfaces   Interprocess communications mechanisms that provide certain high-level services to running processes. Programming interfaces may provide network communication, graphical presentation, or any other type of software service. See also *Interprocess Communications*.

Protected-Mode Boot   A boot process whereby the processor is switched into Protected Mode and the virtual device drivers are initialized.

Protected-Mode Setup   Installing Windows 95 has two parts: Real-Mode Setup and Protected-Mode Setup. Windows 95 completes the install process with the protected mode where it detects hardware, decompresses and installs the files, and makes modifications to the boot record.

Protocol   An established communication method that the parties involved understand. Protocols provide a context in which to interpret communicated information. Computer protocols are rules used by communicating devices and software services to format data in a way that all participants understand. See also *Transport Protocol*.

PSTN   See *Public Switched Telephone Network*.

Public Switched Telephone Network (PSTN)   A global network of interconnected digital and analog communication links originally designed to support voice communication between any two points in the world, but quickly adapted to handle digital data traffic when the computer revolution occurred. In addition to its traditional voice support role, the PSTN now functions as the physical layer of the Internet by providing dial-up and leased lines for the interconnections. See also *Internet, Physical Layer*.

RAS   See *Remote Access Service*.

Real-Mode Boot   After the Master Boot Record step, in the boot process, the Real-Mode Boot checks the system files such as MSDOS.SYS.

Real-Mode Setup   Part of the Windows 95 setup process needs to run in real mode. This is done to ensure that the current system metrics will allow for a successful setup process.

Redirector   A software service that redirects user file I/O requests over the network. Novell implements the Workstation service and Client services for NetWare as redirectors. Redirectors allow servers to be used as mass storage devices that appear local to the user.

Reduced Instruction Set Computer (RISC) A microprocessor technology that implements fewer and more primitive instructions than typical microprocessors and can therefore be implemented quickly with the most modern semiconductor technology and speeds. Programs written for RISC microprocessors require more instructions (longer programs) to perform the same task as a normal microprocessor but are capable of a greater degree of optimization and therefore usually run faster. See also *Microprocessor*.

Registry A database of settings required and maintained by Windows 95 and its components. The Registry contains all the configuration information used by the computer. It is stored as a hierarchical structure and is made up of keys, hives, and value entries. You can use the Registry Editor (REGEDT.EXE) to change these settings.

Remote Access Service (RAS) A service that allows network connections to be established over telephone lines with modems or digital adapters. The computer initiating the connection is called the *RAS client*; the answering computer is called the *RAS server*. See also *Public Switched Telephone Network*.

Remote Procedure Calls (RPC) A network interprocess communication mechanism that allows an application to be distributed among many computers on the same network. See also *Interprocess Communications*.

Remoteboot The remoteboot service starts diskless workstations over the network.

Resource Any useful service, such as a shared network directory or a printer. See also *Share*.

RIP See *Routing Information Protocol*.

RISC See *Reduced Instruction Set Computer*.

Roaming User Profile A user profile that is stored and configured to be downloaded from a server. Roaming user profiles allow users to access their profile from any location on the network. See also *User Profile*.

Router   A network layer device that moves packets between networks. Routers provide internetwork connectivity. See also *Network Layer*.

Routing Information Protocol (RIP)   A protocol within the TCP/IP protocol suite that allows routers to exchange routing information with other routers. A variant of the RIP protocol also exists for the IPX/SPX protocol suite. See also *Transmission Control Protocol/Internet Protocol*.

RPC   See *Remote Procedure Calls*.

Safe Mode   Safe Mode bypasses loading the registry and bypasses the CONFIF.SYS and AUTOEXEC.BAT files. It does not load any network functionality, or protected-mode drivers. It starts Windows 95 in standard VGA and loads HIMEM.SYS, IFSHLP.SYS and the Path from MSDOS.SYS.

SAM   See *Security Accounts Manager*.

SAP   See *Service Advertisement Protocol*.

Scheduling   The process of determining which threads should be executed according to their priority and other factors. See also *Preemptive Multitasking*.

SCSI   See *Small Computer Systems Interface*.

Search Engine   Web sites dedicated to responding to requests for specific information, searching massive locally stored databases of Web pages, and responding with the URLs of pages that fit the search phrase. See also *World Wide Web, Universal Resource Locator*.

Security   Measures taken to secure a system against accidental or intentional loss, usually in the form of accountability procedures and use restriction. See also *Security Identifiers, Security Accounts Manager*.

Security Accounts Manager (SAM)   The module of the Windows NT executive that authenticates a username and password against a database of accounts, generating an access token that includes the user's permissions. See also *Security, Security Identifiers*.

Security Identifiers (SID)   Unique codes that identify a specific user or group to the Windows NT security system. Security identifiers contain a complete set of permissions for that user or group.

Serial Line Internet Protocol (SLIP)   An implementation of the IP protocol over serial lines. SLIP has been largely obviated by PPP. See also *Point-to-Point Protocol, Internet Protocol.*

Server   A computer dedicated to servicing requests for resources from other computers on a network. Servers typically run network operating systems such as Windows NT Server or NetWare. See also *Windows NT, NetWare, Client/Server.*

Service   A process dedicated to implementing a specific function for other process.

Service Advertisement Protocol (SAP)   A NetWare packet broadcast from the server every 60 seconds that contains the server name and the shared resources it has. Windows 95 can also generate a SAP so that NetWare clients will see the Windows 95 box as a NetWare server.

Session Layer   The layer of the OSI model dedicated to maintaining a bi-directional communication connection between two computers. The session layer uses the services of the transport layer to provide this service. See also *Open Systems Interconnect Model, Transport Layer.*

Share   A resource (for example, directory, printer) shared by a server or a peer on a network. See also *Resource, Server, Peer.*

Share-Level Security   The default level of security used in Windows 95. Share-level security is based on passwords assigned to shared resources.

Shell   The user interface of an operating system; the shell launches applications and manages file systems.

SID   See *Security Identifiers.*

Simple Message Blocks (SMBs) A language by which Microsoft servers communicate.

Simple Network Management Protocol (SNMP) A TCP/IP management protocol that manages network hardware such as routers, switches, servers, and clients from a single host on the network. See also *Internet Protocol.*

Site A related collection of HTML documents at the same Internet address, usually oriented toward some specific information or purpose. See also *Hypertext Markup Language, Internet.*

SLIP See *Serial Line Internet Protocol.*

Small Computer Systems Interface (SCSI) A high-speed, parallel-bus interface that connects hard disk drives, CD-ROM drives, tape drives, and many other peripherals to a computer. SCSI is the mass storage connection standard among all computers except IBM compatibles, which use SCSI or IDE.

SMB See *Simple Message Blocks.*

SNMP See *Simple Network Management Protocol.*

Spooler A service that buffers output to a low-speed device such as a printer so the software outputting to the device is not tied up waiting for it.

Subnet Mask A number mathematically applied to Internet protocol addresses to determine which IP addresses are a part of the same subnetwork as the computer applying the subnet mask.

Swap File The virtual memory file on a hard disk containing the memory pages that have been moved out to disk to increase available RAM. See also *Virtual Memory.*

System Monitor Windows 95 tool to monitor performance statistics on the remote workstation.

System Policy   Used to control what a user can do and the user's environment. System policies can be applied to a specific user, group, a computer, or all users. System policies work by overwriting current settings in the Registry with the system policy settings. System policies are created through the System Policy Editor. See also *Registry, System Policy Editor.*

System Policy Editor   A utility found within the System Tools group used to create system policies. See also *System Policy.*

TAPI   See *Telephony Application Program Interface.*

Taskbar   The bar at the bottom of the screen that replaces the Task Manager in previous versions of Windows. The Taskbar holds buttons representing running programs as well as the Start menu button. Used to switch between running programs and choose the Start menu.

TCP   See *Transmission Control Protocol.*

TCP/IP   See *Transmission Control Protocol/Internet Protocol.*

TDI   See *Transport Driver Interface.*

Telephony Application Program Interface   TAPI is a standard way for programs to interact with the telephony functionality in Windows 95.

Templates   ASCII files that correspond to subkeys and values in the Registry. Template files (.ADM files) are used in creating system policies.

Thread   A list of instructions running in a computer to perform a certain task. Each thread runs in the context of a process, which embodies the protected memory space and the environment of the threads. Multithreaded processes can perform more than one task at the same time. See also *Preemptive Multitasking, Program.*

Throughput   The measure of information flow through a system in a specific time frame, usually one second. For instance, 28.8Kbps is the throughput of a modem: 28.8 kilobits per second can be transmitted.

Token Ring The second most popular data link layer standard for local area networking. Token Ring implements the token-passing method of arbitrating multiple-computer access to the same network. Token Ring operates at either 4 or 16Mbps. See also *Data Link Layer*.

Transmission Control Protocol (TCP) A transport layer protocol that implements guaranteed packet delivery using the Internet Protocol (IP). See also *Transmission Control Protocol/Internet Protocol, Internet Protocol*.

Transmission Control Protocol/Internet Protocol (TCP/IP) A suite of network protocols upon which the global Internet is based. TCP/IP is a general term that can refer either to the TCP and IP protocols used together or to the complete set of Internet protocols. TCP/IP is the default protocol for Windows NT.

Transport Driver Interface (TDI) A specification to which all Window NT transport protocols must be written in order to be used by higher-level services such as programming interfaces, file systems, and interprocess communications mechanisms. See also *Transport Protocol*.

Transport Layer The OSI model layer responsible for the guaranteed serial delivery of packets between two computers over an internetwork. TCP is the Transport layer protocol for the TCP/IP transport protocol.

Transport Protocol A service that delivers discrete packets of information between computers in a network. Transport protocols may operate at the Data Link, Network, Transport, or Session layers of the OSI stack. Higher-level, connection-oriented services are built upon transport protocols. See also *Transmission Control Protocol/Internet Protocol, NetBIOS Extended User Interface, Transport Layer, Internet Protocol, Transport Control Protocol/Internet Protocol, Internet*.

UNC See *Universal Naming Convention*.

Uniform Resource Locator (URL)   An Internet standard naming convention for identifying resources available via various TCP/IP application protocols. For example, `http://www.microsoft.com` is the URL for Microsoft's World Wide Web server site, while `ftp://gateway.dec.com` is a popular FTP site. A URL allows easy hypertext references to a particular resource from within a document or mail message. See also *Hypertext Transfer Protocol, World Wide Web.*

Universal Naming Convention (UNC)   A multivendor, multiplatform convention for identifying shared resources on a network.

UNIX   A multitasking, Kernel-based operating system developed at AT&T in the early 1970s and provided (originally) free to universities as a research operating system. Because of its availability and ability to scale down to microprocessor-based computers, UNIX became the standard operating system of the Internet and its attendant network protocols and is the closest approximation to a universal operating system that exists. Most computers can run some variant of the UNIX operating system. See also *Multitasking, Internet.*

User-Level Security   A method by which Windows 95 shares its resources by granting rights to existing users and groups from an NT or NetWare server.

User Profile   Used to save each user's Desktop configuration.

Username   A user's account name in a logon-authenticated system. See also *Security.*

Virtual Machines   Windows 95 uses virtual machines to fool programs into thinking that they have exclusive access to all system hardware.

Virtual Memory   A Kernel service that stores memory pages not currently in use on a mass storage device to free up the memory occupied for other uses. Virtual memory hides the memory swapping process from applications and higher-level services. See also *Swap File, Kernel.*

Volume   A collection of data indexed by directories containing files and referred to by a drive letter.

Web Browser An application that makes HTTP requests and formats the resultant HTML documents for the users. The preeminent Internet client, most Web browsers understand all standard Internet protocols. *See also* *Hypertext Transfer Protocol, Hypertext Markup Language, Internet.*

Web Page Any HTML document on an HTTP server. See also *Hypertext Transfer Protocol, Hypertext Markup Language, Internet.*

Win16 The set of application services provided by the 16-bit versions of Microsoft Windows: Windows 3.1 and Windows for Workgroups 3.11.

Win32 The set of application services provided by the 32-bit versions of Microsoft Windows: Windows 95 and Windows NT.

Windows for Workgroups 3.11 The 16-bit version of Windows for less-powerful, Intel-based personal computers that includes peer-networking services.

Windows 95 The current 32-bit version of Microsoft Windows for medium-range, Intel-based personal computers; this system includes peer-networking services, Internet support, and strong support for older DOS applications and peripherals.

Windows Internet Name Service (WINS) A network service for Microsoft networks that maps NetBIOS names to IP addresses, facilitating browsing and intercommunication over TCP/IP networks.

Windows NT The 32-bit version of Microsoft Windows for powerful Intel, Alpha, PowerPC, or MIPS-based computers; the system includes peer-networking services, server-networking services, Internet client and server services, and a broad range of utilities.

WINS See *Windows Internet Name Service.*

Workgroup   In Microsoft networks, a collection of related computers, such as a department, that don't require the uniform security and coordination of a domain. Workgroups are characterized by decentralized management as opposed to the centralized management that domains use. See also *Domain*.

Workstation   A powerful personal computer, usually running a preemptive, multitasking operating system like UNIX or Windows NT.

World Wide Web (WWW)   A collection of Internet servers providing hypertext formatted documents for Internet clients running Web browsers. The World Wide Web provided the first easy-to-use graphical interface for the Internet and is largely responsible for the Internet's explosive growth.

Write-Back Caching   A caching optimization wherein data written to the slow store is cached until the cache is full or until a subsequent write operation overwrites the cached data. Write-back caching can significantly reduce the write operations to a slow store because many write operations are subsequently obviated by new information. Data in the write-back cache is also available for subsequent reads. If something happens to prevent the cache from writing data to the slow store, the cache data will be lost. See also *Caching*, *Write-through Caching*.

Write-through Caching   A caching optimization wherein data written to a slow store is kept in a cache for subsequent rereading. Unlike write-back caching, write-through caching immediately writes the data to the slow store and is therefore less optimal but more secure.

WWW   See *World Wide Web*.

X.25   Standard that defines packet-switching networks.

X86 Ring Architecture   The x86 architecture supports multiple levels of processor provided protection for running programs. These levels are called Rings. Transitioning between Rings uses a lot of time and system resources. In order to increase speed and reduce errors, Windows 95 uses only two Rings in the x86 architecture, Ring 0 and Ring 3.

Index

Note to the Reader: First level entries are in bold. Page numbers in bold indicate the principal discussion of a topic or the definition of a term. Page numbers in *italic* indicate illustration